Knowing More, but Accomplishing What?

Developing Approaches to Measure
the Effects of Information-Sharing on
Criminal Justice Outcomes

Brian A. Jackson, Lane F. Burgette, Caroline Stevens, Claude Messan
Setodji, Erinn Herberman, Stephanie Ann Kovalchik, Katie Mugg,
Meagan Cahill, Jessica Hwang, Joshua Lawrence Traub

For more information on this publication, visit www.rand.org/t/RR2099

This project was supported by Award No. 2013-IJ-CX-K001, awarded by the National Institute of Justice, Office of Justice Programs, U.S. Department of Justice. The opinions, findings, and conclusions or recommendations expressed in this publication are those of the authors and do not necessarily reflect those of the Department of Justice.

Library of Congress Cataloging-in-Publication Data is available for this publication.
ISBN: 978-0-8330-9899-3

Published by the RAND Corporation, Santa Monica, Calif.
© Copyright 2017 RAND Corporation
RAND® is a registered trademark.

Cover: *GettyImages/Thinkstock*

Support RAND
Make a tax-deductible charitable contribution at
www.rand.org/giving/contribute

www.rand.org

Preface

The sharing of information among criminal justice and public safety agencies has been a central focus in the years since the September 11, 2001, terrorist attacks. Although the threat of terrorism and the desire to strengthen homeland security efforts at all levels of government have been central drivers for recent investments in data-sharing, making data available across jurisdictional boundaries can contribute to everyday criminal justice efforts as well. Programs and systems that provide access to data locally, regionally, and nationally about crimes, individuals with outstanding warrants, and other information have existed for decades and are viewed as important to both the effectiveness and efficiency of criminal justice efforts. Such sharing is also intended to reduce the potential for governmental boundaries to inhibit those efforts, because criminals frequently do not limit their activities to the jurisdiction of a single law enforcement agency.

Although there are high-profile success stories in which data-sharing assisted in solving cases or apprehending criminals, systematic efforts to measure data-sharing's effects on criminal justice outcomes have been relatively rare. Because the sharing of information is not an end in itself, linking sharing to better outcomes in a rigorous way has proven difficult. As a result, policy debate regarding sharing efforts—which have significant monetary costs and raise concerns about effects on citizen privacy and individual rights—has been hampered by a lack of objective data.

This research effort, sponsored by the National Institute of Justice, contributes to filling that gap by developing approaches to link the use of a suite of information-sharing tools provided to local, state, and federal public safety agencies in San Diego County by the Automated Regional Justice Information System (ARJIS) to measures of law enforcement outcomes and the bridging of criminal justice efforts across multiple jurisdictions. This report presents an overview of the results of the study, which are described in greater detail in accompanying technical papers cited throughout. This report should be of interest to criminal justice practitioners, policymakers, civil society organizations, and members of the public interested in information-sharing activities for criminal justice and public safety purposes.

RAND Justice Policy

The research reported here was conducted in the RAND Justice Policy Program, which spans both criminal and civil justice system issues with such topics as public safety, effective policing, police–community relations, drug policy and enforcement, corrections policy, use of technology in law enforcement, tort reform, catastrophe and mass-injury compensation, court resourcing, and insurance regulation. Program research is supported by government agencies, foundations, and the private sector.

This program is part of RAND Justice, Infrastructure, and Environment, a division of the RAND Corporation dedicated to improving policy- and decisionmaking in a wide range of policy domains, including civil and criminal justice, infrastructure development and financing, environmental policy, transportation planning and technology, immigration and border protection, public and occupational safety, energy policy, science and innovation policy, space, and telecommunications.

Questions or comments about this report should be sent to the project leader, Brian A. Jackson (Brian_Jackson@rand.org). For more information about RAND Justice Policy, see www.rand.org/jie/justice-policy or contact the director at justice@rand.org.

Contents

Figures and Table

Figures

Table

Summary

The sharing of information among law enforcement and other public safety agencies has been a central focus of national policy over the past two decades. The September 11, 2001, terrorist attacks were a central driver of efforts to increase sharing, but such efforts were already well under way as part of traditional law enforcement and criminal justice activities. The primary goal of sharing is to give public safety practitioners the information they need to be effective; for example, the data may help connect the dots regarding a potential security threat or contribute to solving a string of property crimes occurring in multiple jurisdictions.

Although there is broad consensus in the criminal justice community that information-sharing is valuable, efforts to measure its effects on performance have been few and far between. Anecdotal success stories of cases in which data from sharing systems were critical to cracking a case or quickly stopping a crime in progress are easy to identify. But even the collection of multiple such success stories does not provide a comprehensive picture of how better data affect criminal justice outcomes overall. Information-sharing systems have substantial monetary costs and can raise concerns about the effects of the collection and dissemination of the data they contain on citizens' privacy and individual rights. An educated debate about those costs requires a rigorous assessment of the systems' benefits.

The Difficulty of Linking Information-Sharing to Criminal Justice Outcomes

A central driver for the limited measurement of how information-sharing systems affect outcomes is that better data can have wide-ranging and diverse effects in criminal justice practice. For instance, better data could allow a police chief to make better strategic decisions about how to deploy officers to fight crime, potentially having effects on observed crime rates. Such data could contribute to investigations by allowing detectives to identify a suspect more quickly—or, conversely, to rule out suspects that they might have otherwise had to contact and interview. Better data could provide directly actionable tactical information to officers on the street, letting them know that the person they are about to cite for illegally parking near a school has an outstanding warrant or is a sex offender who is not supposed to be in the area at all. It is also true that more information is not *always* better, because swamping someone in data—even correct and objectively useful data—can create information overload and actually hurt performance. This complexity has meant that a significant number of past efforts to assess information-sharing systems have been based on user perceptions of the systems' value, relying on the people who use the systems to reflect the many and varied effects that better data can have on their performance.

Although assessments by users can be an important part of evaluation, they have limits—and thus are not sufficient for a fully informed policy debate on this topic. But the reality that better data can have many different effects means that efforts to get at the effects of sharing directly have to be designed to reflect that complexity. As a result, developing a method to measure the benefit of an information-sharing system requires developing multiple measures that provide different pieces of the picture. Analyzing accepted measures of police department performance—such as case clearance rates (i.e., the percentage of cases in which a perpetrator is arrested) or overall crime rates—is a starting point to gauge whether more data-sharing helps improve those measures. Other possible measures include the speed or probability of arrests or of officers locating and interviewing a suspect. As in some previous efforts to assess information-sharing, productivity is another part of the picture—whether the additional data help officers do more in less time. Because a key goal of these systems is building a bridge between public safety agencies that are responsible for geographically or otherwise separate jurisdictions, developing measures that can assess whether using the systems affects collaboration among agencies or has an effect on criminal behavior that moves across those boundaries is also an important piece of the puzzle.

Designing Measures for Real-World Law Enforcement Activities

Even though it is possible to develop logical measures of the different ways that better data can affect police work, measuring those effects must take on the additional complexity that these systems function within existing organizations with existing approaches to doing their jobs. As part of this effort, we conducted interviews with a convenience sample of users of a major regional information-sharing enterprise of multiple systems managed by the Automated Regional Justice Information System (ARJIS) in San Diego County about how the sharing tools ARJIS provides affected the way the users worked. Those interviews revealed great variability in how the data systems affected how different public safety practitioners performed their tasks. In some cases, single users of the systems (whether analysts or officers) served as conduits of information from the systems to others (e.g., participants in a task force they supported), meaning the benefit of the information-sharing systems might be transferred from those users to officers who appeared to not be using the systems at all. There were also differences in whether officers relied more on data from the cross-jurisdictional sharing systems or from their department's own system, meaning that the effects of cross-jurisdictional sharing might be apparently increased or decreased for individual users. Users also cited the possibility of information overload in some instances, validating other studies that have shown such effects. The feedback emphasized that efforts to design measures for how these systems affect criminal justice outcomes must take into account these types of complexities. To be as rigorous as possible, analysis must capture the potential for variation in user roles, ways data might be used that would not be reflected in user logs, how data could affect different tasks, and the possibility for negative effects. This could be done by framing measures that try to simplify and isolate the complications or that internalize their varied effects.

Three Sets of Measures Linking Sharing to Criminal Justice Outcomes

In collaboration with ARJIS and informed by insights from its users, we tested three approaches for measuring the effects of information-sharing on criminal justice outcomes. The goal was method development; this was not an independent evaluation of ARJIS but rather a collaborative study combining the capabilities of researchers and criminal justice practitioners. Each approach to measurement was distinct in that it looked at separate sharing features or tested different measurement strategies. Though not addressing the complete universe of sharing effects, the measures complement one another and provide distinct pieces of an overall picture of sharing effects. Because this effort examined a sharing system that was already well established, we were limited in our evaluation designs; for example, it was not possible to use randomization or other approaches that would have provided the strongest causal information. The results should therefore be interpreted with caution; they are measurements of correlation, not causation—although the measures do provide a generally consistent picture of the effects of different types of data-sharing. Next, we describe the three sets of measures we tested.

The Officer Notification System—Records to Flag Important Information

One feature ARJIS provides is the ability for authorized users to create records via the Officer Notification System (ONS) that flag key information about an individual, address, or vehicle. These records are designed to make sure that an officer is made aware of particularly critical information for safety or other purposes. ONS records can be viewed by other officers, dispatchers, and other authorized users when they make matching queries and, in some ARJIS applications, are displayed more prominently than other ARJIS records in search results. One task that uses these records is sex offender registration, where ONS records provide officers with information on the registered offenders' conditions of release and other relevant data. We examined a group of registered offenders with ONS records and compared them with a group of registered offenders without such records. We examined measures regarding multi-agency involvement in the registered offenders' supervision, as well as measures for individuals' interactions with the criminal justice system.

On both types of measures, analysis showed different effects for the group with ONS records. On multi-agency involvement, individuals with ONS records were 75 percent more likely than those without them to have a recorded contact with law enforcement (these events include citations, field interviews, crime cases in which an individual is cited as being a suspect, or arrests) from more than one agency. And the time to the next contact with a different agency was shorter as well: 1.3 years for the group with ONS records versus 1.7 years for the control group without such records. Furthermore, individuals with ONS records were more likely to be associated with multi-agency involvement in in the six months before and after a crime case (14 percent more likely than the control group) or an arrest (10 percent more likely). On the criminal justice outcome measures, individuals with ONS records had higher probabilities and shorter times for several pairs of events. For example, individuals with ONS records were 32 percent more likely than those without to be arrested after a crime case for which they were a suspect, and it happened much more quickly (with a median difference of more than three years). The probability and timing of field interviews (an investigative activity) after a crime case had even larger differences between the groups: Interviews with flagged individuals were more than twice as likely and happened a median of more than seven years sooner.

"Be on the Lookout" Notifications—Distribution Lists to Gather Information from Other Officers or Trigger Law Enforcement Action

Among the ARJIS tools that link users of the system to each other are "be on the lookout" (BOLO) notifications. Officers can subscribe to different categories of BOLO email distribution lists and access them on desktop computers, in vehicles, and on ARJIS-connected mobile devices. Officers use these notifications tactically (e.g., disseminating information to other officers about someone with an outstanding warrant) and investigatively (e.g., asking other users whether there are cases in their jurisdictions similar to a case the requester is working to solve). The notifications are used differently agency-to-agency and even among users. BOLOs can also be used for non-suspect or non–crime case purposes, such as rapidly disseminating information about a missing person to officers in other jurisdictions to broaden the search, although our evaluation did not include those uses.

To explore the effects of BOLO notifications, we looked at counts of crime cases and arrests recorded in ARJIS systems for suspects in cases in which BOLOs were used either tactically or for information-gathering purposes and compared those counts with matched cases in which such notifications were not used (a matched case was defined as one with the same highest offense, agency, and police beat and that occurred within a month of the case in which the BOLO was used). The strongest association that was measured for the BOLOs in our sample was a significant increase in crime cases associated with suspects from BOLO cases compared with other cases (between 0.25 and 0.9 additional cases, on average). This is consistent with the use of BOLOs to identify crime series across jurisdictions. Although our analysis was suggestive that BOLO notifications increased arrests for cases in which a BOLO was used, those effects did not meet the requirements for statistical significance.

Information-Sharing System Usage and Involvement in Cross-Jurisdictional Policing
Another potential outcome of improved information-sharing is addressing the fact that criminal activity can cross jurisdictional boundaries. Previous studies have shown that "traveling criminals" represent a significant percentage of crime perpetrators and that offending in multiple jurisdictions may reduce the likelihood that the offenders will be apprehended. Although multiple factors could be at play in making it difficult to apprehend traveling criminals, cross-jurisdictional information-sharing might help reduce any advantage resulting from offending in different geographic areas.

Because of differences in the way jurisdictions record their data, it was not possible to definitively link crime cases in one jurisdiction to arrests in another in a large-scale and automated way. As a result, we had to build a data set that linked crime cases with identified suspects to arrests by varying criteria, which gave us a set of cases for analysis. The strongest criterion that suggested that a case and a cross-jurisdictional arrest are related was documentation in the arrest record submitted to ARJIS that the arrest was related to a warrant originating in another jurisdiction. If a suspect's cross-jurisdictional arrest after a crime case was *not* associated with a warrant in the record submitted to ARJIS, we matched cases and arrests that were close in time by other factors, such as the charges involved. We then looked for a relationship between the amount of an officer's use of ARJIS systems (e.g., did the officer do lots of ARJIS application searches or very few) with the officer's number of apparent cross-jurisdictional arrests.

Looking across the entire sample of potential cross-jurisdictional arrests (including arrests based on a warrant and all matched case-arrest pairs), an increase from zero to ten queries per month in the ARJIS systems included in our analysis was associated with, on average, an estimated 0.028 more monthly cross-jurisdictional arrests per officer (from 0.164 arrests to 0.192 arrests). In other words, such increased ARJIS use increased the average estimated probability of making a cross-jurisdictional arrest in a given month from 11.7 percent to 13.1 percent (with both results highly statistically significant). With a narrower definition of a cross-jurisdictional arrest (that is, narrowing the matching criteria), the effects were in the same directions but got weaker. At the most restrictive—looking at cases that involved warrants—an increase from zero to ten queries was associated with the average monthly number of cross-jurisdictional arrests increasing from 0.044 to 0.048, while the estimate for the probability of making a cross-jurisdictional arrest in a given month was much smaller and lost statistical significance. As with all of the analyses discussed in this document, we emphasize that the data are observational, and at least part of the observed association may reflect confounding due to unobserved factors.

Conclusions

Responding to limitations in current approaches to assess the effects of information-sharing on criminal justice outcomes, we developed a suite of approaches to measure such effects at the user, offender, and case levels. By identifying situations in which the amount of information-sharing at each of those levels differed, we were able to identify strong correlations between sharing and case outcomes, timelines, and inter-jurisdictional policing activities. While readers should remain cognizant of the limits of the results presented in this study, together, the results provide consistent pieces of a picture demonstrating the contribution of data-sharing to improved criminal justice outcomes. Sharing through ARJIS systems was associated with greater multi-agency involvement with specific registered offenders, which is consistent with such systems' goal to reduce the effect of jurisdictional boundaries on agency activities and effectiveness. Data-sharing and BOLO notifications were associated with increases in the number of crime cases connected to suspects—an important outcome given the role of serial offenders in an area's total crime burden. The amount (or dosage) of use of data-sharing systems—measured across a large user population—was correlated with numbers and probabilities of cross-jurisdictional arrests.

Beyond demonstrating approaches to assess current information-sharing efforts, this study also identified actions that could be taken going forward. Given trends toward more emphasis on using data to improve the effectiveness and efficiency of criminal justice agencies, our results suggest ways that new data systems could be better designed (or innovations that could be implemented in existing systems) to make the sort of analysis done here easier. In an era of tight budgets at all levels of government, making it easier and cheaper to measure information-sharing systems' contributions is likely to become more rather than less important.

Other technology trends—such as adoption of officer-worn cameras that might capture location and other data, as well as advances in analytics that may make it easier to link data to beneficial outcomes—have the potential to help break down some of the measurement roadblocks this analysis encountered to enable even better and more-rigorous measurement of how data help practitioners across the justice system do their jobs better. Thinking now about which data should be recorded and kept to make that sort of high-resolution analysis of the effects of criminal justice data on outcomes possible would make a down payment on a future in which justice agency leadership, analysts, and decisionmakers will know more than just that sharing data is generally valuable. They will be able to understand which data, delivered where, and delivered how contribute most to criminal justice practitioners' ability to do their jobs safely and well and to achieve the complicated set of goals that society expects them to achieve.

Acknowledgments

The authors would like to acknowledge Pam Scanlon of the Automated Regional Justice Information System (ARJIS), whose efforts and contributions helped frame the overall project and informed the various analyses we performed. We would also like to acknowledge the contributions of Konstantin Anufreichik, Vu Huynh, and Yong An of ARJIS's programming and analytical staff, whose efforts to extract data and facilitate the analysis were critical to the successful completion of this project. We would also like to thank the officers and leadership of the departments that participated in the mobile device deployment evaluation, whose willingness to provide data was critical for that portion of the study. Martin Zaworski kindly shared with us survey materials and data from his previous study of ARJIS, which contributed to the design of our data-gathering. We would also like to acknowledge Steve Schuetz and Bill Ford of the National Institute of Justice for their efforts over the course of the effort. For their helpful comments during the peer review of this report, we acknowledge Andrew Morral of RAND and David L. Carter of Michigan State University.

Abbreviations

ARJIS	Automated Regional Justice Information System
BOLO	be on the lookout
DNA	deoxyribonucleic acid
IT	information technology
LPR	license plate recognition
N-DEx	National Data Exchange
ONASAS	Officer Notification and Smart Alerting System
ONS	Officer Notification System
RISS	Regional Information Sharing System
RMS	record management system
SRFERS	State, Regional, Federal Enterprise Retrieval System
TACIDS	Tactical Identification System

CHAPTER ONE

Introduction

Information-sharing became a central element of the policy debate about U.S. home-land and national security after the September 11, 2001, terrorist attacks (9/11). In the report of the commission examining those attacks, some of the key recommendations focused on the need for security organizations to be able to "connect the dots" and to limit the tendency for boundaries between organizations at the federal, state, and local levels to impede information flow (National Commission on Terrorist Attacks upon the United States, 2004).

While domestic security and the threat of terrorism were frequently the focus of debate about information-sharing, such sharing is just as important for other functions in the criminal justice system—specifically, data moving across jurisdictional bound-aries so that a police officer in one area can benefit from what other agencies know about a suspect, so that court proceedings or plea negotiations about a citizen accused of a crime are supported by all relevant data, and so that information can be exchanged between justice agencies (e.g., correctional systems) and organizations outside of gov-ernment that help achieve justice outcomes (e.g., mental health providers that assist citizens after release from incarceration).

The term *information-sharing* has been used in a variety of ways during the policy debate, referring to very specific and tangible transfers of data between users, as well as to more-diffuse mechanisms for sharing expertise or promoting collaboration between people or entities with different skills and capabilities (reviewed in Jackson, 2014). This range of uses of the term—covering efforts as well defined as information technology (IT) systems that link databases between organizations and fusion centers or task forces that bring together professionals from different agencies to jointly solve problems—emphasizes that it is the *use* of shared information that matters. It is not that expertise or data are theoretically available to criminal justice or security prac-titioners but that the practitioners can actually use the data to do their jobs better, faster, or more effectively.

In considering how information-sharing is linked to outcomes that the nation expects from justice or security organizations, examination of what sharing accom-plishes can start within a single organization or agency, where such efforts seek to ensure that individuals are aware of and can access organizational data relevant to their roles and can use that information effectively. For example, in a single police department, crime data could flow outward to individual officers in the field so that they have a fuller picture of criminal activity in their area of responsibility. Similarly, data could flow inward to help organizational leadership assemble a detailed and up-to-date picture of crime in the jurisdiction to inform strategic decisions. Initiatives in police departments across the country have focused on information moving in both directions; for example, some tactical-level systems push real-time crime data to computers in squad cars or to mobile devices that officers carry, while some strategic-level CompStat processes are designed to give leaders at all levels actionable insights into crime trends or events in their jurisdictions.

However, given the structure and organization of criminal justice in the United States (as well as the broader U.S. homeland security enterprise, which includes multiple federal, state, local, and tribal agencies with many distinct missions), individual organizations are often not the focus of information-sharing efforts. Instead, sharing efforts often seek to move data across the myriad boundaries that exist between similar agencies in different jurisdictions (e.g., neighboring police departments), agencies in interdependent criminal justice roles (e.g., law enforcement, courts, and corrections agencies), or among agencies with related but distinct missions (e.g., national security, law enforcement, public health, and nongovernmental entities). In a cross-agency context, data and other sharing might enable

- a police officer in one agency to act to resolve a crime that occurred in another jurisdiction
- agencies to assemble patterns of behavior that enable the disruption of organized criminal or terrorist activities
- organizations to apply data from other disciplines to better achieve their own missions (e.g., a public health agency using crime data to better target interventions aimed at illegal drug use).

In the more than 15 years since 9/11, efforts aimed at facilitating information-sharing have expanded in the United States, building on activities and infrastructure that were already in place well before those attacks occurred. There is a wide variety of U.S. systems and initiatives designed to share data across the criminal justice and homeland security enterprise. A comprehensive review of such systems would be a difficult task and is beyond the scope of this report,[1] but the following three examples illustrate the diversity of such efforts:

- *Automated Regional Justice Information System (ARJIS).* ARJIS is an agency that provides a suite of regional information-sharing applications in the San Diego

---

[1] For a review of information available on the range of information-sharing initiatives and the challenges associated with fully understanding the variety of in-progress efforts, see Jackson, 2014.

County metropolitan area, connecting more than 80 criminal justice agencies at multiple levels of government.

- *Regional Information Sharing System (RISS).* RISS, founded in the 1970s, comprises six regional information-sharing systems that—taken together—cover the entire United States and provide connectivity among member agencies to share data on intelligence, investigations, and gang activity, as well as officer safety–related information.
- *National Data Exchange (N-DEx).* N-DEx is a national-level system, built and managed by the Federal Bureau of Investigation, that provides criminal justice practitioners across the country with access to shared data from other jurisdictions (e.g., police departments in other states or localities).[2]

Other efforts exist across the country at the state and local levels or designed around the specific information-sharing needs of particular areas (e.g., the National Capital Region surrounding and including Washington, D.C.). These sharing initiatives have been implemented in a range of forms, including purpose-designed information systems acting as a bridge between multiple agencies, direct connections (enabled by data and technology standardization) between independent agencies' record and communication systems, or processes in which data are passed back and forth between entities on a regular basis.

Particularly for information-sharing across jurisdictional boundaries, the policy focus on improving sharing has resulted in the creation and expansion of organizations to facilitate and improve sharing and initiatives to help address the organizational, technical, and other barriers that can get in the way of sharing efforts. For example, at the federal level, the Intelligence Reform and Terrorism Prevention Act of 2004 created the Office of the Program Manager for the Information Sharing Environment, which develops standards; coordinates across organizations; participates in working groups; and helps address security, privacy, and other barriers to sharing (Information Sharing Environment, undated). Though specifically focused on national security and terrorism concerns, the office is linked with sharing efforts focused on criminal justice more broadly, including the Global Justice Information Sharing Initiative (Global) and its Criminal Intelligence Coordinating Council (U.S. Department of Justice, undated). Global, a federal advisory committee with participation from multiple independent organizations across the criminal justice sector, develops information-sharing toolkits; manages initiatives related to technology, policy, and standards; and provides a venue and structure for collaboration and coordination. Federal grant programs (including in the criminal justice and homeland security areas) have funded efforts to improve

---

[2]   Participation in N-DEx has increased rapidly in the past few years. In 2013, approximately 4,200 agencies were participating in the system (Mitchell, 2013), and according to 2016 data provided to the authors by N-DEx, that total had increased to approximately 5,800 (Kasey Wertheim, N-DEx Project Manager, personal communication, October 2016).

sharing, which provides a resource stream for investment in both technology and organizational capability. Practitioner, research, and other stakeholder organizations outside of government also have initiatives, committee structures, and activities aimed at improving information-sharing (e.g., Hunter, 2009; SEARCH, undated; International Association of Chiefs of Police, undated).[3]

While it would be difficult to estimate the resources that have been spent putting information-sharing systems and initiatives in place and supporting their operation, national expenditures on information-sharing have been considerable. Efforts focused on examining funding for information-sharing at the state and local levels (e.g., Harrison, 2005) have tabulated costs in individual states ranging from hundreds of thousands to tens of millions of dollars, which suggests that total expenditures across the United States are at least in the tens of millions of dollars per year. Efforts to tabulate information-sharing expenditures within the U.S. Department of Homeland Security as part of a congressional examination of that department's fusion centers (some of which would double count portions of the state and local estimates that were funded with federal grant dollars) produced an estimate between $150 million and $200 million per year (Permanent Subcommittee on Investigations, 2012). A later multi-agency analysis that included state, local, tribal, territorial, and some private-sector expenditures produced estimates between $250 million and $330 million per year (Inspectors General of the Intelligence Community, Department of Homeland Security, and Department of Justice, 2017, p. 46). Accepting the limits of existing efforts to tabulate sharing expenditures, the results are nonetheless sufficient to demonstrate that the scale of government resources devoted to information-sharing reaches into the hundreds of millions of dollars per year.

Given the opportunity costs associated with such a significant expenditure, there is a clear need to know what these investments in information are yielding in order to support an educated debate about priorities and policy. If the investments' benefits in the criminal justice and homeland security spheres are commensurate with their costs, current or even expanded efforts to increase data- and other sharing may be warranted. But if not, understanding the cost-effective level of investment in these functions is necessary so that resources can be redeployed to achieve other policy goals. And despite strong support for information-sharing activities in the criminal justice and homeland security sectors, systematically linking information-sharing to its outcomes is often very difficult, which hurts policymakers' ability to make appropriate decisions in this area.

---

[3]   For a review of the variety of information-sharing issues, technical concerns, and many of the policy efforts aimed at addressing them in the law enforcement sector, see Hollywood and Winkelman, 2015.

CHAPTER TWO

How Can We Measure the Effects of Information-Sharing?

In considering security and criminal justice agencies' missions, the value of greater sharing of information may seem self-evident. Investigating crimes; detecting threats; and making decisions about charging, sentencing, or taking other criminal justice actions involve myriad decisions, the quality of which are related to the completeness, relevance, and currency of the data available to inform them. For individual cases, it is often easy to see the benefit of data flowing from one department to another. For example, a 2016 article on N-DEx described a case in which a detective—even as he was still being trained on using the sharing system—ran a search relevant to an active case and found that his suspect had recently been arrested in another state (Wertheim, 2016a). Similar instances of cases that might not have been solved or solved as quickly without such systems provide compelling anecdotal evidence for the value of data-sharing.

However, while such examples can be the starting point for evaluation, they are not sufficient to be its end point. Even for individual cases, we can ask deeper questions. Was a case that appeared to be unsolvable without data from an information-sharing system actually impossible to crack without it? Or was the effect of the system really about speed (that is, the case could be cracked much faster using the new tool)? If that was the case, how much faster? Although minutes can make a difference in some criminal incidents, being able to crack a case in hours that otherwise would have taken weeks would be a more substantial effect than cracking a case in two hours that otherwise would have taken three. An individual case can provide a dramatic narrative about how better data-sharing can improve outcomes, but for investments whose costs can run into the tens of millions of dollars, it is important to measure how often such situations occur. If a multimillion-dollar system makes a definitive difference on only one case a year, we would likely judge it very differently than if it made such a contribution many times a day.

Evaluating benefits across all the cases and tasks that the justice system performs is particularly important because such systems have costs that go beyond the tax dollars supporting the data entry, computer infrastructure, and devices that get the information to potential users. More information flowing to officers or investigators could produce an effect familiar to anyone who has used a modern Internet search engine— having to wade through many results that the search algorithm retrieved but that were

5

not relevant to the problem at hand. If that occurs, an officer may have to spend more time looking for the relevant data, and even if finding the data might translate to better outcomes for some cases, the added burden may cause other cases to get less attention. Information flowing from one place to another also has implications for the citizens who are its subjects, and depending on how the sharing systems are designed, the information might lose its context—and its meaning and implications might therefore shift—as a result of being shared (Jackson et al., 2017). The accuracy of data is also a concern. The broad sharing of wrong information has the potential to magnify even a single clerical error into a life-changing event for a person or a situation in which law enforcement wastes considerable time pursuing an innocent person while a guilty one is at large. A full accounting of the effects of information-sharing therefore requires looking at benefits and costs across many cases, not just high-profile success stories.

A Relatively Limited Evaluation Literature on Information-Sharing Systems

Because information-sharing has been such a high-profile component of justice and security debate for several decades before and especially since 9/11, analysts and researchers have explored ways to measure the effects of sharing on the functioning and outcomes of agencies. Doing so is not straightforward, because information is not being shared simply for the sake of sharing but with the intent of doing something else better. As a result, measuring how much data have been entered into a system, whether the system has lots of users who run lots of searches, or the amount of information that is available to members of different organizations that was not before does not answer the fundamental question of interest. These are essentially intermediate steps that—while related to the desired outcome—are not the same as that outcome. Instead, they are measures of process or outputs and do not make the final link between those steps and what users are doing with the outputs to achieve criminal justice or security goals. Many of the efforts to assess information-sharing systems at the federal level have been characterized (e.g., by the U.S. Government Accountability Office) as focusing on processes and outputs rather than outcomes.[1]

There have been some—though comparatively few—efforts to collect quantitative data on information-sharing system performance and to link the data to the outcomes they are intended to produce.[2] Hauck (2005) studied a law enforcement instant mes-

---

[1]   For reviews of such efforts, see, for example, Larence, 2008, 2011; U.S. Government Accountability Office, 2010, 2012, 2013a, 2013b, 2014; U.S. Department of Homeland Security, 2012. There is also a substantial literature focused on this type of evaluation, which does have a role to play in the management of information-sharing and other IT systems.

[2]   Early in the application of IT to policing, studies asked users about outcome improvements and included measures of use of state or federal databases (which provide cross-jurisdictional information-sharing). For example,

saging system and sought to connect its use to arrests, case characteristics, and other measures (which showed mixed results).[3] Koper et al. (2015)'s study on technology applications in law enforcement evaluated an internal law enforcement social media platform that was intended to improve data-sharing across shifts and actually saw detrimental effects on robbery case clearance rates after implementation. Other efforts (by both public policy analysts and academics) have examined information-sharing systems using mixed methods or more-qualitative approaches. These have included collection of user perception data (i.e., not whether use of the system can be shown to have positive outcomes but whether users believe that it does) and survey methods that seek to link use of information-sharing to individual knowledge (Information Sharing Environment, 2012; Zaworski, 2005; Chen et al., 2002; Scott, 2006; Bean, 2009).[4] Past efforts' reliance on process and indirect measures of outcomes is understandable given the challenge in linking sharing to outcomes (e.g., crime reductions or improved case clearance rates) and disaggregating its effect from other factors.[5] Without clear ways to make that linkage, user perceptions of utility may seem like the best proxy, relying on the expertise of users to make their own assessments even while acknowledging the limitations of that approach for strength of the evaluation conclusions.

The Comprehensive Regional Information Sharing Project was one of the most comprehensive efforts to develop more-standard ways of thinking about and evaluating the effects of cross-jurisdictional sharing. The effort examined several regional sharing systems and noted that, at that time, "there [was] no established set of metrics for regional law enforcement [sharing systems]" and most statistics that were collected were "useful for daily operations . . . [but did] not necessarily help determine how effectively a system meets law enforcement needs" (Noblis, 2007b, p. 3-4). Survey data collected during that effort suggested that some agencies did collect some data

---

Ioimo and Aronson (2003) showed case clearance effects and increases in queries to state and federal databases as a result of the implementation of mobile computing in a law enforcement department. Wellford and Cronin (1999) found that database searches related to weapons and suspects in homicide cases were related to the probability of case closure.

[3] More-substantial work seeking to link information-sharing efforts to outcomes was focused on task force organizations—where staff from multiple agencies worked together on common tasks; however, such efforts combine sharing with joint action, so they represent a somewhat different case than computer-based sharing systems (reviewed in Jackson, 2014).

[4] In earlier work when IT use was spreading in the criminal justice system, such user perception studies sought to link the extent of system use to outcome effects. For example, looking at detectives, Danziger and Kraemer (1985, p. 200) linked use of computing to users' reports of "cases unworkable without computing, arrests where computing assisted, clearances where computing assisted, linkages of [individuals] in custody to uncleared cases," and more-general "informational benefits from computing."

[5] At its most basic, this is an evaluation or experimental design challenge. Many of these complications can be minimized if information-sharing can be manipulated; for example, when a new system is being implemented, its introduction could be staged to allow maintenance of both an experimental and a control group. However, for systems that are already in place, such manipulations are not possible.

internally on their participation in regional information-sharing systems (Taylor et al., 2006, p. 37). Almost two in ten such agencies collected success stories of system use, and some agencies more systematically collected information that had the potential to connect sharing more directly to outcomes of interest, including time to solve crimes (15 percent), use of "link analysis transactions to link search keywords to investigations or crimes solved" (12 percent), and "improved community outreach feedback/public trust—possibly measured by increased leads from the community" (15 percent) (Taylor et al., 2006, p. 37). Building on their survey and other data, the authors proposed measuring such variables as arrests of individuals who committed crimes in one jurisdiction but lived in another; the linkage of records from different agencies during investigations; how frequently the sharing system enables users to identify leads, make arrests, or clear cases; and efficiency measures, such as time savings and productivity increases (Noblis, 2007a, pp. 3-4–3-7).[6] In that effort, collecting data for many of the measures would require users to be routinely surveyed, so implementation would face the same problems and concerns about burden that earlier qualitative evaluation efforts have encountered.[7]

The shortfalls in rigorous evaluation approaches have limited policy debate about these efforts. For example, in 2012, an investigative committee of the U.S. Senate issued a report critical of some homeland security sharing efforts (which included dissecting some cases viewed as success stories and called into question the appropriateness of that characterization) (Permanent Subcommittee on Investigations, 2012). Others disagreed with the committee's conclusion (e.g., International Association of Chiefs of Police, 2012). The absence of solid approaches to measure the effects of information-sharing on outcomes of interest limited the ability of both critics and proponents to support their arguments and to have a productive debate on these systems and capabilities.

Logically Linking Information-Sharing to Outcomes for Developing Measures

For criminal justice information-sharing, the fundamental outcomes of interest are reductions in crime and increases in the appropriateness of the actions taken by criminal justice agencies, in pursuit of a safe and healthy society. Focusing on law enforce-

---

[6]   The Comprehensive Regional Information Sharing Project effort also defined a wide range of measures related to system operations and processes, such as the quality and currency of data included in the system. For our effort here, we do not focus on such measures—although their effect would be captured, to some extent, in outcome measures for systems. For example, if a sharing system delivered a significant amount of incorrect or out-of-date data, it would presumably have limited (or even negative) effects on law enforcement outcomes.

[7]   Geerken et al. (2008) identified measures for sharing efforts, including total arrests; increases in case clearance within defined periods; and process measures, such as counts of queries made in the system.

ment, these broader societal goals are pursued through such tasks as patrolling neighborhoods to deter criminal activity, responding to and investigating criminal incidents, and seeking to build and maintain connections with communities to ensure that law enforcement can serve them effectively and draw on them as partners and collaborators to help achieve common goals.

Research effort in the criminology and public administration fields has been devoted to developing clear outcome measures for police organizations.[8] Examples of the measures include crime rates, clearance rates (i.e., the proportion of crimes in which an arrest is made or that are resolved in another way), response times to calls to the police for assistance, and citizens' views of the police and their willingness to contact the police for assistance when they are victims of crime. Sparrow (2015, p. 1) also describes "measures of enforcement productivity," such as arrest counts or the number of interactions between officers and citizens—including Terry stops (often referred to as stop-and-frisk searches), which are arguably not outcomes but relate to investigation and case clearance. The effectiveness of police in addressing crime or solving community problems can also increase community satisfaction and reduce citizen fear of crime, which are critical outcomes reflecting the fundamental goals policing is intended to achieve. Improvement in measures of the effect of police activity on external behavior (e.g., deterrence of crime), the effectiveness of such activity (e.g., solving more crimes), and the efficiency of such activity (e.g., solving them more quickly) may therefore contribute to improvement in broader (and potentially more societally important) measures. Reflecting the complexity of the environment in which police departments operate and how approaches to achieve one outcome (e.g., crime reduction) can affect others (e.g., citizen satisfaction with the police might increase or decrease as a result of the tactics used to achieve crime control), there is consensus that assessment must consider multiple measures rather than single metrics in isolation.[9] With respect to this effort on information-sharing, we focus on measures of police efficiency and effectiveness, understanding that sharing-driven improvements in those areas may have cascading effects on broader measures as well.

In considering the effects of information-sharing on police work, a starting point is to consider how better information can improve officers' efforts. Each person at all levels of a department makes numerous decisions—how to allocate resources and time, who to arrest, and so on—that affect how desired outcomes are achieved. In prin-

---

[8]   This literature is reviewed in Moore and Braga, 2003; Davis, 2012; and Sparrow, 2015.

[9]   Although the focus in this report is measuring information-sharing effects on law enforcement outcomes, these systems could have effects on important process measures for agencies as well. In one frequently cited example, risks to officer safety may be reduced when officers have more-complete data about the people and locations they encounter. For instance, when officers can look up information about an address before responding, they may learn that the location has been a site of violent crime or violence against police and can therefore be better able to respond safely.

ciple, better information can make it possible to make better decisions and, therefore, improve *effectiveness*.

Better decisions could turn on *data availability*—that is, a decisionmaker may choose to do something that he would not have done had he not had the data. For example, a police chief may decide to put more officers in an area because a more accurate picture of the crime that is occurring there identified the need, or an officer may arrest someone who she would not otherwise have known had an open warrant. At the same time, a better decision could involve *not doing something* that otherwise might have been done. Reversing the previous examples, more-accurate data could allow the police chief to remove officers from an area and redeploy them to more-urgent roles or tasks. And more-complete data about an individual's history with the criminal justice system might lead an officer to choose to do something other than arrest him—even if his behavior might have justified doing so (e.g., the officer may learn that the subject has a mental illness that causes him to react aggressively, so rather than arrest the subject, the officer refers him to treatment). Such actions might be reflected in increases in citizen satisfaction but not in arrest or clearance numbers.

The benefits for decisionmaking and effectiveness can also come from improvements in *data quality*. For example, local data might be wrong, and the alternative data available from a sharing system can call out that fact, limiting the risk of the decisionmaker acting on wrong information. But there are other factors besides accuracy that can make data more or less useful for informing criminal justice action. For instance, data should be complete—particularly if any missing information about a person or incident is critical for understanding. Timeliness or currency is another facet of quality; accurate but outdated data may have little value. Other problems that can affect criminal justice data sets include inconsistency (e.g., individuals being included in data sets with different spellings of their names or dates in different formats) and duplicate records. Access to more data through sharing could either help address or create additional complexity, so issues in any of these data-quality areas could affect decisions.

But, as Geerken and colleagues explain, the "quality of decision-making is very difficult to measure because it cannot be easily defined as a quantity of something (which is, of course, what a measure is). For example, higher quality judicial decisions in setting bonds is not indicated by higher or lower average bonds, but by more *appropriate* bonds" (Geerken et al., 2008, p. 18, emphasis in original). This is the first challenge to crafting meaningful metrics for information-sharing: Better information could push simplistic measures of criminal justice processes or outputs in different directions, and, thus, relying on those measures alone risks producing confusing or uninformative results. Returning to the earlier example, better information could increase or decrease arrests by individual officers for different reasons, even setting aside that it may not be entirely clear whether an increase or decrease is a good or bad development. As a result, just counting total arrests would not be the best measure, because what a change in one direction or the other meant in terms of the sharing system would be difficult to interpret. On the other hand, using how fast contact is made with suspects identified in a criminal case would be less ambiguous. There is a clearer line between how quickly effective action can be taken on identified crimes and the desired agency outcomes than there is between total arrests and those outcomes. And the former measure would capture the fact that rapid contact with suspects could have benefits for containing escalating situations and more rapidly clearing cases by arrest, as well as more rapidly resolving suspicion of individuals who turned out to be innocent of any wrongdoing.

Like other IT systems, an information-sharing system can have beneficial effects even when benefits are not seen in decision quality. A major effect of these technologies can be practitioner *efficiency*. That is, even when practitioners get the same data that they did before (and thus the quality of any individual decision is unaffected), they may get the data faster or with less effort. If the time saved enables them to do more— for example, a detective can work two cases in the time that it would have previously taken to work one—there will still be benefits to criminal justice outcomes overall.[10] The outcome measures that efficiency improvements would affect would depend on how the newly available time was used—although if increases in efficiency were offset by resource reductions or staffing cuts, they might not be observable in departmental outcomes but would be seen in process measures, such as organizational budgets.

However, efficiency is not an inevitable outcome of information-sharing systems. If the data available in different systems are in conflict, time and effort may be required to resolve the contradiction. If the alternative would be to make decisions based on incorrect local data, that time and effort will likely be justified but could have an efficiency price. In addition, access to shared data, by definition, increases the volume of information available to analysts and decisionmakers. Such an increase creates the potential for information overload, which could slow or confuse decisionmaking, which may cost rather than benefit efficiency and possibly reduce decision quality.

This "Goldilocks quality"—the idea that having too little or too much information can be a problem, but getting just the right amount results in the greatest benefit—is the second major challenge for developing measures of the effect of sharing on criminal justice outcomes. This effect has been recognized for many years as potentially creating a benefit versus information quantity curve like that shown in Figure 2.1, where the top of the inverted U-shape reflects the ideal region for effectiveness (for a multidisciplinary review of this literature, see Eppler and Mengis, 2004). While it is important to know that a system is actually being used (because building a network does not matter if nothing is flowing to users via that network), simply knowing this fact is not informative. If use of the system crowds out rather than enables productive activity or if the information delivered swamps users to the point that they cannot make decisions at all, the system will not be valuable.

---

[10] In practice, these two effects will be mixed—because getting data to an investigator or officer faster (efficiency) may also help him or her identify and successfully apprehend the perpetrator (effectiveness).

Figure 2.1
Law Enforcement Effectiveness Versus Information Quantity

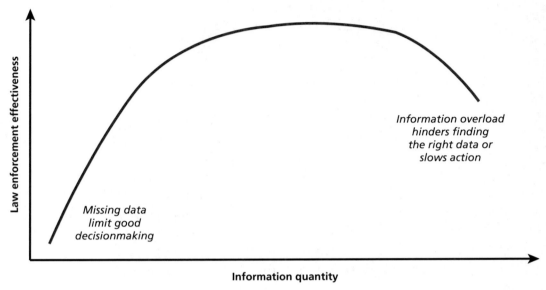

Developing appropriate measures therefore requires addressing these two challenges as much as possible: (1) limiting the risk that measures combine different effects of data on decisionmaking in confusing ways and (2) capturing the inherent quality that both too little and too much information can cause negative outcomes.

Evaluating information-sharing systems also must address the complication that sharing tools can contribute to a wide variety of criminal justice decisions, and the tools' potential effects on those decisions can vary. To help better define this challenge, we use three examples: the simplest case, in which sharing one piece of information triggers a well-defined action; an intermediate case, in which the aggregation of data enables a decision to act; and the broadest case, in which shared data shape the nature (but not the occurrence) of a criminal justice decision.

Starting with a relatively simple case, *information can trigger action by making decisionmakers aware of the need to act* when they have the opportunity to do so. For a law enforcement officer, this information might come from a "be on the lookout" (BOLO) notification that provides a photo of a suspect in a recent criminal incident or that makes them aware of an outstanding warrant on an individual the officer might encounter. The effect of sharing in these cases is essentially an all-or-nothing proposition: Having data in the hands of the person in a position to act will allow action, and not having the data will mean the opportunity to act is missed. Measures of the probability of arrest or how quickly an arrest was made would be useful because, in this case, the effect of sharing should only increase that probability (in contrast with the more-complex examples discussed previously, where sharing could simultaneously increase and decrease numbers of arrests). Measuring how such notifications affect the probability or timing of arrests would also capture the Goldilocks quality of information-sharing—because if alerts were issued on so many cases that recipients were overloaded and stopped paying attention, then the measures would be expected to gradually revert to the measures for comparable cases. This type of simple, tactical information-sharing—whose effects would be expected to be observable at the individual case level—would also be straightforward to assess even for systems that have already been implemented, assuming comparable groups of cases in which the sharing was and was not done could be identified.

Solving a crime by collecting evidence to identify a suspect or detecting planning and preparation for a terrorist or other incident is another—and likely the most familiar—task enabled by information-sharing and is somewhat more complicated than a simple "alert to act" described in the previous paragraph. Here, *sharing contributes to decisionmakers assembling multiple pieces of information, thus enabling a decision to be made or an action taken* (e.g., to arrest a suspect to clear a case or to act to disrupt a planned criminal incident). As in the "alert to act" case earlier, this intermediate case is somewhat all or nothing in character because one key data point can be critical to crack a case or detect a plot, and whether an investigator has that piece of data may determine success or failure.[11] However, this example is also affected by the first two challenges outlined earlier: In an investigation, more useful information could increase the likelihood of solving a crime, but it also might speed or slow the investigation. And information that is not relevant or high quality might slow the process even more or hurt the chance of success—and, if the task at hand is detecting a future terrorist plot, delay and failure might be one in the same. As a result, measuring the effects of sharing here requires more-nuanced metrics.

In analysis that focuses on measuring effects at the level of individual users of the system, just looking at a change in productivity would be hard to interpret. For example, if a user is clearing fewer cases the more she uses the system, that could reflect that the information being provided is producing negative effects (e.g., using the system is taking too much of her time, the information is confusing and diverting her efforts), or the information may be enabling her to produce better cases by weaving together all the data available, but it takes more time to do that. As a result, without some companion measure of the quality of the user's output—for example, how the strength of the cases she is involved in changes as her use of the shared data increases—it is tough to discern whether the effect is good or bad. Speeding or increasing the probability of completing some intermediate steps of the process (e.g., time to identify, locate, and contact identified suspects or witnesses) might be less ambiguous, but even such data would need careful scrutiny. For instance, if information-sharing provided many pos-

---

[11] Or, to apply the popular metaphor of connecting the dots to detect a future criminal incident or solve a past crime, there may be one critical dot (or a small number of dots) that makes the picture make sense.

sible people to contact who were unproductive in solving a crime, it could slow the investigation even if each person could be contacted very quickly.

Looking at the individual case level simplifies measuring the effects of data-sharing to some extent, although unambiguously teasing out the effects remains difficult. For a crime case, such measures as probability of clearance through arrest (or the time to do so) would internalize the effects of both of the challenges described earlier—because clearance by arrest is a relatively unambiguous positive outcome of a legitimate crime case, and the Goldilocks quality of having too little or too much information would be captured in the timeline required for clearance. All other factors equal, one would expect access to more information to increase the probability of case clearance, but it might do so in ways in which the analysis timeline mattered. For example, over a short timeline (e.g., a week), the clearance probability of cases in departments with lots of access to data-sharing might appear lower than that for comparable cases in departments without it, because of the time required to access and use the data. But over longer timelines (e.g., a month), the advantages of more information access might build and cause the probabilities to diverge as expected. Shorter timelines would make it easier to disentangle efficiency effects, while longer timelines would "net out" all the different effects on overall justice outcomes. But even in this case, linking measures like case clearance to quality is important because, for example, it would be an unambiguously negative outcome if a sharing system enabled more-certain or more-rapid case clearance by facilitating the arrest of people for crimes they did not commit.

Shared data can also inform decisions at the highest strategic or operational levels in a criminal justice agency, where the data's effects may be less obvious. In this broadest case, information often is not triggering a new decision; instead, the *data shape the details of a decision that would have been made in any case.* In the patrol allocation example discussed earlier, the decision is whether one area should have more police presence than another, not whether to have police presence at all. Aggregation of crime data from many adjacent jurisdictions to create an up-to-date picture of crime is an example of sharing enabling this type of decisionmaking (in the context of agencies' CompStat processes, for example). Predictive analytics to support policing is another example, because—at their most basic—such techniques try to fuse data to give a better picture of future crime and opportunities for policing to prevent it.

Unlike the simple and intermediate cases, where the question was how to appropriately distinguish the different mechanisms for how information-sharing affects decisions and outcomes, in this broader case, distinguishing them appears almost impossible. Continuing with the same example, information overload might delay changes in reallocation of patrol resources, but measuring the marginal opportunity cost of that delay would be difficult unless the evaluation was able to do a controlled experiment with and without the shared data. However, at the strategic level, some of the difficulty in relating the effects of sharing (e.g., more or more likely arrests) to the organizational goals could be lessened, assuming that the department has a set of metrics that appropriately capture those goals.[12]

Teasing out the effects of sharing on decisions and actions at these different levels will obviously be most straightforward when a new sharing initiative is put into place, so that circumstances before implementation can be compared with those after the new data are available. When that can be done—and, ideally, experimental techniques (such as randomization) can be used—there would be greater clarity in measuring effects. Yet even the ideal of a randomized implementation may not address all concerns, because users may need time to learn how to use a new information system effectively, potentially delaying observation of any effect, beneficial or not.[13]

For systems that are already in place, it is more complicated to measure how decisions and actions are affected by information-sharing. Some analysts have suggested attempting to artificially create a comparison by eliciting from users how they would have to do their tasks in the absence of the sharing system—and using what they report to anchor thinking about the system's effects.[14] While such a qualitative approach can be valuable, the evidence it provides—like that of anecdotal success stories for system use—is much weaker than directly measuring the effects of data-sharing on outcomes. To pursue a quantitative measurement for already-implemented systems, we therefore must think about information-sharing in dose-response terms—where a case, practitioner, or decision process is viewed as a target of "treatment" with data from the system, and effects can be compared for different dosages. If the dosage is different for different treatment targets and the range of dosages goes high enough, such an approach could also make it possible to discern information overload, if it occurs. Individual officers might use the system more or less, and therefore comparisons across a continuum of use could see both efficiency and effectiveness effects. And suspects or convicted offenders may be entered into the system in different ways (or different information-sharing features may be relevant to different people), making it possible to distinguish different outcomes. For cases, investigating officers might use the system more or less, or different sharing methods might be applied to some cases but not others. But across different dosages, the quality—not just quantity or speed—of the outcome should ideally be tracked to make sure that what is being measured is really what matters.

---

[12] Because of the state of performance measurement in policing today, this is far from a certainty. Currently, there is no both accepted and broadly applied set of performance metrics for policing that fully capture the complexity of the crime prevention, crime resolution, community relationships, societal health, social service, and other myriad facets of the modern law enforcement mission set.

[13] Studies of commercial firms from as early as the 1990s have recognized lags in the appearance of benefits of new investments in IT systems.

[14] In previous work, others named this "but for" analysis because it asks what users' jobs would look like "but for" the use of the information-sharing system (described conceptually in Noblis, 2007b, p. 2-6 and defined as an analysis approach in Geerken et al., 2008).

These approaches and ideals provided the foundation for our effort to work with an existing information-sharing system and develop approaches to measure the effects of sharing on criminal justice outcomes. Although we were able to implement many of these concepts, the collision of theory and practice showed that achieving some of the desired outcomes was still an ideal and provided insights into how sharing systems could better capture data to enable improvement in measurement and evaluation going forward.

CHAPTER THREE

Developing and Testing Measures with the Automated Regional Justice Information System

ARJIS is a regional Joint Powers Agency that allows real-time law enforcement applications and data to be shared among 82 local, state, and federal criminal justice agencies in San Diego County, California. ARJIS serves as the region's hub for information-sharing; officer notification; and the exchange, validation, and real-time uploading of many types of public safety data. ARJIS membership comprises more than 4,900 authorized public safety personnel, representing a comprehensive cross-jurisdictional and multidiscipline user base. By relying on a variety of committees led by elected officials, law enforcement executives, officers, and crime analysts, the ARJIS governance structure promotes information-sharing and cooperation at all levels.

ARJIS is responsible for major public safety initiatives, including wireless access to photos and other critical data in the field, mapping, crime analysis tools, and an enterprise system of applications that help users solve crimes and identify offenders. In this capacity, ARJIS has developed replicable open source technical solutions, policies, and governance guidelines that have been leveraged at agencies across the nation. ARJIS incorporates the standards, guidelines, and best practices established through the Global Justice Information Sharing Initiative, including compliance with the Global Justice XML Data Model and National Information Exchange Model standards, as well as use of a service-oriented architecture approach to maximize information-sharing efficiency. In addition, ARJIS relies extensively on its users to provide needs assessments, requirements analyses, business use case scenarios, testing, and feedback on technology initiatives.

In this research effort, RAND collaborated with ARJIS to develop approaches to measure the effects of information-sharing on criminal justice outcomes. The goal was method development; this was not an independent evaluation of ARJIS but rather a collaborative study combining the capabilities of researchers and criminal justice practitioners. Because ARJIS includes a variety of different features and sharing mechanisms, it provided a real-world case study in which to experiment with measuring the effects of different types of data-sharing. Different tools provided by ARJIS can be grouped into classes based on how the sharing is triggered: by individual users searching for data ("user pull"), automatically by the system ("system push"), or by users reaching out to other users through the connections provided by the system ("user to user"). Table 3.1 summarizes the ARJIS tools.

As part of the formative efforts for the study, we interviewed a convenience sample of 29 users of ARJIS systems. We identified interviewees largely by having agency representatives nominate candidates, so our initial pool likely reflected individuals whom those representatives felt used and were knowledgeable about ARJIS sharing applications. During the interviews, we also asked initial participants for their suggestions of others who would have valuable input—whether or not those individuals were frequent users of ARJIS systems. Approximately three-fourths of the interviewees were agency nominees, and the remainder were added to the sample by participant suggestion. Participants were drawn from the full range of organization types that use ARJIS sharing applications, including federal organizations and San Diego County law enforcement and corrections agencies. The participants also spanned a wide variety of job titles, roughly split among detectives; crime analysts; police officers, corrections officers, and federal officers; and officers in managerial roles. (Detectives made up slightly more than a quarter, and managerial officers made up less than a quarter.)

Table 3.1
Summary of ARJIS Tools

Class	Tool or Feature	Description
User pull	User query of linked databases (State, Regional, Federal Enterprise Retrieval System, or SRFERS)	Federated query of multiple databases across the region, state (e.g., the California Law Enforcement Telecommunications System, or CLETS), and nationally (e.g., Nlets, or the International Justice and Public Safety Network)
	Officer Notification System (ONS) records	Records created by authorized users to flag key information about an individual (e.g., sex offender status, officer safety concern), address, or vehicle when other officers or users perform a matching query
	In-field identification of individuals from photo databases (Tactical Identification System, or TACIDS)	Biometric matching of photos with booking mug shots to assist in establishing the identity of individuals who have been detained based on reasonable suspicion and are lacking and/or not forthcoming with their identification or who appear to be using someone else's or false identification
System push	Officer Notification and Smart Alerting System (ONASAS) automated alerts	Coupled with ONS records, ONASAS allows an authorized user to enter a subscription for a specific record in the system (e.g., a person or vehicle) and receive an automated email or text message notification when another user accesses that record
User-to-user	"Be on the lookout" (BOLO) notifications	Email notifications sent to subscribing users requesting information, seeking to identify individuals (e.g., from photos at a crime scene), or flagging individuals for interview or arrest
	Task force email distribution lists	Email distribution lists for members of task organizations working on common problems (e.g., violent crime task forces)

The goal of the qualitative interviewing was to gather information that would provide insights into how use of the sharing tools was connected to criminal justice outcomes, and how the ways that practitioners used the tools might affect the ability to directly associate use with outcomes. The full list of interview questions is included in the appendix to this report, but the questions sought to explore

- how users worked
- users' reliance on different ways to get information to do their jobs, and the extent that information came from outside their home agencies
- the types of tasks information systems were used to perform, and the types of data that were particularly useful in those tasks
- the perceived effects of systems on users' productivity, and whether there were any challenges or issues in using the systems
- how a situation in which ARJIS sharing applications had been particularly helpful would have been resolved without the availability of cross-jurisdictional information-sharing.[1]

The ARJIS users we interviewed varied considerably in the circumstances in which they worked, with variation even among practitioners with similar roles. Interviewees included patrol officers who worked alone, with a partner, or as part of multiperson units or task forces. Among the analyst participants, some worked alone and others worked as part of larger units. Detectives showed similar variation as patrol officers, with some reporting working mostly on their own, some with partners, and others as part of stable teams focused on specific crimes (e.g., a homicide task force). This variation flagged a potential challenge for assessing the effects of individual officers using information-sharing systems. If an officer works on his own all or most of the time, then his access to data through sharing systems should be reflected in his individual outcomes in solving cases, making arrests, or other activities. But if an officer works as part of a group, one member of the group might be the primary user of the sharing tools (e.g., a dedicated crime analyst serving a task force) for the benefit of all of the members; therefore, there will be officers whose work has benefited from the sharing system but who appear (based, for example, on login or search history logs) to not be users of the system. *In designing evaluation strategies, this type of variation in work models must be considered lest analyses build in biases that risk distorting the outcomes measured for the systems.*

The interviewees also reported reliance on different information sources, as well as variation in the amount of cross-jurisdictional information they used in their work. Although ARJIS provides access to data and sharing capabilities across San Diego County, it is not the only source of information for criminal justice practitioners in the

---

[1] This set of questions attempted to lead the participants through the "but for" analysis described in Chapter Two.

area. Individual agencies have their own records systems (which feed ARJIS systems) that their members can use. Other information query tools are also available; for example, a tool provided by the San Diego Sherriff's Department is the primary route for accessing up-to-date warrant information. As part of our qualitative data-gathering, we asked the interviewees whether they used ARJIS's or their own agencies' systems more in executing their responsibilities. Of those who provided clear relative comparisons, approximately 60 percent said they used ARJIS tools more than their agencies' systems, and 40 percent indicated they used ARJIS tools less than those systems. While this demonstrates that use of the cross-jurisdictional systems is prominent for many users, it also demonstrates the evaluation challenge presented when an information-sharing system is not the sole system available to criminal justice practitioners in an area. One driver of these differences in use of interagency versus own agency systems (or potentially a consequence of differences in use) was that participants made vastly different judgments about the importance of interagency data for doing their jobs. When asked what percentage of the information they regularly used came from outside their own agency, responses ranged from 10 percent to 90 percent, with a median response of 55 percent. *In designing evaluation strategies for interagency information-sharing systems in particular, the effects of alternative sources of information must be considered.* The effects of use of a "home agency" system would be expected to be more important for larger jurisdictions (e.g., the San Diego Police or Chula Vista Police Departments in this study) that have more internal data than smaller agencies.

As would be expected, when we asked users about the types of tasks they used data to perform, responses varied by role; for example, analysts reported developing crime maps and doing statistical analyses of data from ARJIS systems, while detectives and line officers reported using data to identify people who were not willing to provide identification or who provided partial or false information. The system can help support identification not just of suspects in crime cases but also victims or witnesses. Interviewees cited such other tasks as using photos in the system for lineups, using cross-jurisdictional information on individuals' past contacts with the criminal justice system, and locating outstanding warrants. *In designing evaluation strategies, the effects of information-sharing for different tasks may be quite different, potentially requiring different types of users to be examined separately.* For example, data from a neighboring jurisdiction may produce a crime map that provides more insight for a chief making staffing allocation decisions, resulting in more crime deterrence (and therefore fewer arrests); however, when the same crime data and descriptions of suspects are provided to patrol officers or detectives, the result may be an increase in arrests. *In addition, because sharing systems can enable intermediate investigative steps, there may be time lags between use and related outcomes.* For example, using the system to discover an outstanding warrant on someone at a traffic stop would result in an immediate arrest, but using the system to identify a victim or witness might advance an investigation but not produce a clearly measurable outcome until later.

Although not all interviewees used ARJIS tools the same amount or for the same things, nearly every respondent credited the tools with increases in their productivity. Some estimated that the tools provided by ARJIS at least doubled their productivity, saving the equivalent of hours a day in effort and enabling more cases to be worked faster. At the same time, when asked about information overload, about two-thirds of the respondents who answered indicated that it could be an issue at times—for example, when searching for more-common names or when presented with many types of records simultaneously. *In designing evaluation strategies, capturing the potential for excessive information to affect performance needs to be captured, rather than assuming that all effects of increased sharing will be positive.*

When asked the hypothetical question of how outcomes of specific incidents (or criminal justice outcomes more broadly) would have been different in the absence of cross-jurisdictional information-sharing, some respondents had difficulty answering because, having had access to the capability for so long, it was difficult for them to envision doing their jobs without it. Other respondents who had experience with alternatives—either from serving in San Diego before ARJIS systems were fully implemented or in other jurisdictions without such systems—could work through the "but for ARJIS, how would the situation have been resolved" analytic process. In such cases, interviewees described the potential for very long timelines to request hard-copy materials from other departments, call or email contacts in other agencies, or manually search records. Interviewees cited the potential for individuals to be charged for only a single crime versus multiple ones (if relevant open cases in other jurisdictions were unknown), for case timelines to change from days to months, and for law enforcement to be forced to make practicality-driven decisions not to investigate some incidents (e.g., property crimes) that would be too labor-intensive without rapid data access. Other respondents were even more pessimistic, wondering how an investigator would know to request records from one of the many jurisdictions in the area if he or she did not already know the records existed; one summarized that "without ARJIS, [investigators] would need to wait for the offenders to get very unlucky, do something stupid, or just stop." *In designing evaluation strategies, these responses emphasize the potential importance of capturing how the availability of data can affect decisions about what to investigate, beyond how data can affect the investigations that are done.* For systems that are already in place, capturing the latter effect can be particularly difficult.

Developing Approaches to Measure Effects of Information-Sharing

At a basic level, measuring the effect of an intervention like information-sharing—whether within single agencies or across agency boundaries—requires differences in the level of the intervention (ideally with all other factors constant) to make it possible to look for differences in outcomes. Thinking of information or system use as a treatment, different dosages should produce different effects (illustrated earlier in Figure 2.1). In the ideal study design, that dosage could be directly controlled and done so in a randomized way, making it possible to establish with statistical confidence that differences in dosage were responsible for differences in outcomes.

Because ARJIS is an established organization providing systems used in day-to-day law enforcement operations, we could not control the dosage directly nor use randomization or other techniques to, for example, allow some officers more or less access to the sharing tools to see how that access would affect their productivity or other variables. As a result, in our effort to develop ways to measure outcome effects of information-sharing, our research team worked with ARJIS technical staff to identify situations that had existing variation in dosages of system use. In some cases, this was akin to looking for natural experiments—where, for reasons outside the study, circumstances created different dosages of information-sharing. In other cases, it was a process of seeing how routine administrative data (e.g., login counts, system logs, and other types of data) could allow us to identify differences that could then be used for analysis.[2]

In looking for differences in dosage, we explored four main options for analysis, each of which might be connectable to criminal justice outcomes in different ways:

1. *Geography.* Geographic divisions may be one level for analysis. Looking at the department level might demonstrate the effects of information-sharing on major strategic decisions (e.g., allocation of patrols for crime deterrence),[3] but doing so is more difficult for an information-sharing system that is already in place than for one being newly implemented.[4] Analyzing geographic subdivisions within one larger department might be more feasible. For example, if Precinct A in a large agency has many heavy users of the sharing system and Precinct B has very few users but the crime types and other characteristics of the two geographic areas are similar, the different dosages of sharing between the areas might be used for evaluation. This approach requires geographic locations for users of the system over time, so the analysis could reflect, for example, an officer from Precinct A being transferred to Precinct B.

---

[2] This effort was itself a learning process in which the team learned lessons about how the types of data that IT systems do and do not routinely record created opportunities for this type of evaluation in some cases and, in others, seriously complicated the effort. We return to those lessons at the end of the report, because they can inform thinking about system design for areas that have not yet implemented information-sharing systems.

[3] The potential value of cross-jurisdictional information-sharing at this level has been recognized for some time. See, for example, Eck, 2002.

[4] The central challenge for departments with existing systems is determining the appropriate comparison or control to assess any performance effect. Given the many differences among separate police agencies, identifying comparable departments (or using analytical methods to construct comparison groups artificially) is difficult.

Geographic areas could be used for assessments based on different outcome measures, and some in particular—including effects on citizen views or willingness to call police—are only meaningful on a geographic basis. When analyzing case clearance, crime events that occurred near the borders of subdivisions with different levels of system use could be particularly informative for assessing system effects.

2. *User.* When outcomes can be connected to specific individuals, dosage of information-sharing could be measured at the user level. For example, a patrol officer who runs many license plates or names of encountered individuals would logically have a greater chance of becoming aware that a vehicle was stolen or that a person has an outstanding warrant than an officer who ran very few plates or names. Variation in dosage at this level is captured very well in administrative data, although using the data for assessment must take into account potential differences in work models (discussed previously) that would make it more difficult to link outcomes to individual users.[5]

3. *Crime case.* Variation in information-sharing dosage could occur at the case level as well. For example, it might be that the details about one case were sent to a multi-agency notification list, while the details about an otherwise comparable case were not. Similarly, an investigator might do many database searches while investigating one crime and do fewer searches for another. Some types of this variation are readily captured in administrative data (e.g., whether a notification on a case was sent to many users), but other types are more difficult to capture. For example, whether the intensity of search on a case is straightforward to determine depends on what data are logged when users run searches (e.g., is the linkage to a specific case recorded) and is compounded by concerns about work models already discussed.

4. *Suspect or offender.* Differences in information-sharing system use with respect to different suspects or offenders could be used to identify effects for a subset of criminal justice outcomes. This analysis option is most relevant for case clearance (e.g., where more searches regarding suspects in a case might lead to investigative success) but might also focus on supervision outcomes in a probation or parole setting. For example, ONS records are an ARJIS feature that make officers who search for an individual aware of key information about the person's past contact with the criminal justice system. When such records are placed on some convicted offenders but not on other similar individuals, the dosage of information-sharing activity on the two groups would be different.

---

[5] Focusing at the user level is also consistent with the observation in other sectors that measuring the effects of IT requires metrics for individuals' use (Devaraj and Kohli, 2003).

Returning to Sparrow (2015)'s discussion of measures for policing, there are a handful of ways that information-sharing might be reflected in changes in performance. Across the different types of law enforcement tasks,[6] changes could be seen in volume (e.g., more arrests or a higher probability of arrest given a crime case), time (e.g., faster case clearance), and effects on quality (e.g., fewer errors or the production of higher-quality cases that are more likely to result in successful resolution in the courts through plea, prosecution, or trial outcome).[7] If information-sharing improves effectiveness at the strategic level, effects might be reflected in lower incidence of crime (e.g., if the data improve police tactics and therefore deter crime more effectively) or improvements in community views of police (e.g., if better data limit disruption or community costs in the course of police activities).

Because reducing the effects that jurisdictional boundaries can have on criminal justice efforts is one of the core goals of information-sharing systems that span multiple jurisdictions, measures that capture the aggregate performance in producing criminal justice outputs or outcomes of multiple agencies simultaneously could also provide insights into the effectiveness of the systems. For example, one measure of the effect of sharing might be the involvement of multiple agencies in a single case or with an individual (during an investigation, parole, or probation supervision), where information-sharing could increase the likelihood, amount, or speed of that multi-agency involvement. Researchers have observed that offenders who operate across jurisdictional boundaries often have a lower probability of apprehension than offenders who limit their criminal activity to one agency's area of responsibility.[8] An absence of such observed differences for criminals operating across jurisdictional lines could also provide evidence for the effect of information-sharing efforts.

Because this research effort was based in a geographic area that has had cross-jurisdictional information-sharing in place for decades, there were not really the large-scale differences in information-sharing dosage available to look at potential strategic outcome effects like the application of data to inform larger-scale decisions about policing, deterrence, or other agency activities or at outcomes like community views of departmental effectiveness. As a result, our effort was pushed to lower levels—focusing

---

[6]   Sparrow (2015) discusses three main classes of tasks: "functional work," in which measures need to capture quantity and quality; "transactional work," in which measures could include volume, speed, accuracy, cost, and satisfaction; and "problem-oriented or risk-based work," in which measures must be customized to assess whether an action is reducing the risk or solving the problem at hand.

[7]   If better information from a sharing system leads to higher-quality cases and arrests, then the dosage of system usage on a case or the extent of use by an investigating officer might be associated with less case attrition as associated arrests move forward through the criminal justice system.

[8]   See, for example, discussion in Lammers and Bernasco (2013), which showed that criminals who spread their crimes over multiple jurisdictional regions (in the Netherlands) had a lower probability of being apprehended than criminals who concentrated their offending. A later study showed that offense specialization reduces probability of arrest, but repeat offending increases it (Lammers, Bernasco, and Elffers, 2012).

on evaluating the effects of information-sharing use for cases, system users, and individuals with contact with the criminal justice system (e.g., suspects, offenders under supervision). At that level, the focus was generally on the amount of time for an event to occur (e.g., arrest of a suspect after a crime case involving that person) or the probability of an event occurring.[9] Examples of the indicators of multi-agency involvement that we explored include the amount of time to involvement with an individual, the extent of that involvement, and an arrest by a member of a one organization for a crime case associated with a different jurisdiction.[10]

Experiments in Outcome Measurement

During this project, we explored a variety of approaches to measure effects from using information-sharing systems. We characterize the effort as a set of experiments in outcome measurement, as not all of them were successful. In some cases, attempts failed simply because of constraints on our ability to access auxiliary data (e.g., specific locations of officer deployment over time) that were necessary to do some analyses. In other cases, limitations in the way data are captured and integrated into the cross-jurisdictional information-sharing systems made it difficult or impossible to explore the effects of a sharing feature or type of system usage. In addition to describing the evaluation experiments that worked, we describe some of these unsuccessful trials where the lessons learned would be useful to others pursuing evaluation efforts.

In the remainder of this section, we describe experiments in which the combination of dosage information and one or more measures made it possible to analyze the relationship between cross-jurisdictional information-sharing and some criminal justice outcomes. In this report, we summarize the measures developed and results of the experiments, and greater detail is provided in technical articles published separately.

The Officer Notification System—Records to Flag Important Information

When an officer searches for information in an encounter with an individual or about a particular address, not all potentially related data are of equal importance. For example, if the owner of a car that has just been pulled over for speeding has a history of violent offenses or violence against officers, it is more important that the officer involved is made aware of that history than of the number of unpaid parking tickets associated with that vehicle. To enable this, ARJIS systems include the ONS application, which makes it possible for authorized criminal justice practitioners to enter a record flagging

---

[9] We could not explore the effects on arrest quality because we could not link the law enforcement information-sharing system with prosecutor or court data during the study.

[10] Building on previous literature that sought to measure efficiency effects of information-sharing, where possible, we also examined the presence of efficiency effects of system use.

critical information. In some ARJIS search tools, these records are more prominently displayed in related query results—for example, in a different text color or at the top of search results. ONS records can be used for a variety of purposes, including notifying officers of safety-related details, requesting information about contacts with a person or address to support an investigation, and sharing information on specific types of registered offenders (e.g., sex offenders, arson registrants, and specific narcotics offenders) and the conditions of their supervision. ONS records fall into the category of "user pull" sharing modes (see Table 3.1) because they are displayed only when a user searches for the related person, address, or vehicle.[11] Although ONS records could trigger user-to-user sharing of information (for notifications related to investigations), the type of record examined in our evaluation experiment pushed information to the user doing the searching, making specific information more prominent and thus reducing the chance it would be missed in reviewing an individual's records when interacting with a police or community corrections officer.[12]

The population examined in our evaluation was registered sex offenders,[13] and ONS records are employed as part of monitoring such registrants. The ONS record can be used to summarize the sex offense penal code(s) and describe the offense(s) an individual was convicted of, the date of his or her most recent registration, the agency of that registration, other types of ONS records (not related to sex offenses), registration requirements, community supervision status and officer information, and residential address (see Kovalchik et al., 2017, p. 279). For the study, we identified more than 5,000 registered sex offenders with ONS records related to their registration status and more than 1,800 registered sex offenders without such records. All individuals who did not have any additional contact with law enforcement during the study were dropped from the sample, leaving approximately 3,900 individuals with ONS records and 581 without them. By doing this, we could compare the nature of law enforcement interactions with individuals in the two groups in an effort to identify possible effects of the presence of an ONS record.

---

[11] ARJIS improved ONS application by adding ONASAS, an automated alerting feature. That feature allows users to subscribe to automated alerts for specific individuals, locations, vehicles, or other records of interest. When an event occurs that is related to a subscribed entity—for example, a new crime case is added for a person or another officer does a search for the license plate of a vehicle of interest—an automatic notification is sent to the subscriber(s) by email or text message. This is a "system push" feature and one that users perceive as useful, as evidenced in our interviews with ARJIS users and in existing literature of user perceptions of similar capabilities in different systems (Lin, Hu, and Chen, 2004). In this study, we attempted to evaluate this feature by comparing comparable cases that had no ONS records, ONS records *without* automated smart alerts, ONS records *with* automated smart alerts, and ONS records *with* automated alerts *that had been triggered* during the study period. Because of data-collection issues (discussed later) that reduced the potential sample size for this experiment, we could not analyze the effects of this feature.

[12] This type of salience feature, in essence, seeks to reduce the chance that information volume or overload causes users to miss important data, thus avoiding the part of the curve that bends down in Figure 2.1.

[13] The complete analysis is documented in Kovalchik et al., 2017.

One set of measures we tested focused on the role of this ARJIS information-sharing tool to break down barriers between different jurisdictions. The data set for each registered sex offender included all the interactions he or she had with the criminal justice system during the study period (these events include citations, field interviews, crime cases in which the individual was cited as being a suspect, and arrests). Our measures for multi-agency involvement were whether different agencies became involved more rapidly in criminal justice events for individuals with ONS records versus those without and whether events involving different agencies were more closely clustered in time (that is, multi-agency involvement was more densely grouped together) for registered offenders with ONS records versus those without. To get a measure of criminal justice outcomes, we focused on timing—that is, whether pairs of events (e.g., a field interview or arrest after a crime case) occurred faster for individuals with ONS records versus those without.

On both types of measures (multi-agency involvement and criminal justice outcomes), analysis showed different effects for the group with ONS records. On multi-agency involvement, registered offenders with ONS records were 75 percent more likely than those without them to have a recorded contact with law enforcement from more than one agency. And the time to the next event with a different agency was shorter as well: 1.3 years for the group with ONS records versus 1.7 years for the control group without such records. In addition, individuals with ONS records were 14 percent more likely than the control group to have contact with multiple agencies in the six months before and after a crime case and 10 percent more likely in the six months before and after an arrest.

On the criminal justice outcome measures, offenders flagged with ONS records had higher probabilities and shorter times for several pairs of events. For example, offenders with ONS records were 32 percent more likely than those without to be arrested after a crime case in which they were a suspect, and it happened much more quickly (with a median difference of more than three years). The probability and timing of field interviews (an investigative activity) after a crime case had even larger differences between the groups: Interviews with flagged offenders were more than twice as likely and happened a median of more than seven years sooner.

Because the two groups of offenders were not generated randomly, the differences between them must be interpreted cautiously. There are clear correlations, but we cannot make strong conclusions that ONS records caused the differences. The observed effects may be driven by systematic differences between the two groups that we could not observe; for example, if the offenders with ONS records were higher risk than those without, such a difference could result in similar effects. To help address that issue, we took a subset of the criminal justice outcome measures and compared each offender with an ONS record to him- or herself in the periods before and after the ONS record was added. When we did so, significant differences existed on many of the measures (e.g., the likelihood of a field interview after a crime case was even larger for the individuals when they had ONS records), but some differences dropped out of the analysis (e.g., there was no longer a significant difference in the likelihood of arrest after a crime case). This "within offender" comparison has its own limitations—most importantly, any changes in the individuals' offense profiles over time would affect their contact with police or corrections personnel—but the persistence of differences adds to the picture of how ONS records potentially affect outcomes.

"Be on the Lookout" Notifications—Distribution Lists to Gather Information from Other Officers or Trigger Law Enforcement Action

Among the ARJIS tools that link users of the system to each other are BOLO notifications. Officers can subscribe to BOLO email distribution lists, which serve to replace older modes of providing tactical information to officers on the street, such as handing out tip sheets at pre-shift roll-call briefings. The notifications are also a more dynamic way to query colleagues in other agencies for assistance on cases. An example of a tactical application of BOLOs is when officers use them to disseminate identifying information on a high-profile suspect for whom a warrant was recently issued. For information-gathering, officers may use BOLOs to circulate a suspect's photo to seek assistance in identifying that person or may ask other investigators whether there are cases in their jurisdictions similar to a case the requester is working to solve. BOLOs can also be used for non-suspect or non–crime case purposes, such as rapidly disseminating information about a missing person to officers in other jurisdictions to broaden the search. Officers can subscribe to different categories of BOLO email distribution lists and can access the resulting notifications on desktops, in vehicles, and on ARJIS-connected mobile devices. BOLOs feature prominently in several information-sharing success stories cited by ARJIS users, such as identifying suspects rapidly, defining crime series, and informing large numbers of officers about time-sensitive situations (e.g., ongoing child abductions).

When considering how to measure BOLO notifications' effects on crime cases, several effects might be observable.[14] Effects at the case level (e.g., a BOLO issued about a crime case might increase the chance it was cleared) and at the suspect level (e.g., a BOLO citing a person as a suspect might increase the chance that person is arrested) essentially converge—because a case would be cleared through the arrest of a suspect. By enlisting the help of more officers in an ongoing case, BOLOs might decrease the time for specific events to occur (e.g., time to interview a suspect). However, because BOLOs are also used to identify crime series across jurisdictional boundaries, their use might also increase the number of cases cleared via a single arrest or the number of charges or distinct crime cases linked to a particular suspect. In our analysis, we did not examine uses of BOLO notifications that were not related to crime cases (e.g.,

---

[14] The complete analysis of the measurement of BOLO effects is available in Burgette et al., unpublished manuscript.

location of missing persons), because it would be more difficult to identify the effects of such use using data available from ARJIS systems.

From our interviews with users of ARJIS systems, it is clear that the use of BOLO notifications differs from agency to agency, with some making greater use of the feature than others. The "treatment" of a case or suspect with a BOLO is therefore not random, so we had to identify an appropriate comparison set for cases for which BOLOs were used. For a group of crime cases for which BOLOs were issued (just over 300 cases, with BOLOs issued between January and April 2014), we identified comparison cases that matched on highest offense, agency, and beat and that occurred within one month of the BOLO case. Then, for suspects connected to the cases with associated BOLOs, we looked at criminal justice events (citations, field interviews, crime cases, and arrests[15]) recorded in ARJIS systems in the 180 days before and after the BOLO was issued and compared those events against the same measure for suspects in the matched cases for which no BOLO was issued. (The focal crime cases of the BOLO and matched control were not included in either the before or after measures.)

Of the more than 80 agencies that use information-sharing tools provided by ARJIS, only a subset—though a geographically broad subset—contribute data to the systems (see Figure 3.2). As a result, only arrests from data-contributing agencies are reflected in this analysis. However, users from all the agencies can subscribe to BOLO email distribution lists. Therefore, some crime cases and arrests by those agencies may be related to BOLOs but are not reflected in this analysis, meaning our estimates of the effects of BOLOs could be conservative underestimates of their actual effects.

In an effort to further control for any differences that the matching process did not address between suspects in BOLO cases and suspects in the comparison cases, we compared the pre-post differences in each case. Because different cases had different numbers of suspects associated with them, we did the analysis two ways—for one, we normalized by the number of suspects in each case, and for the other, we did not.

The strongest effect measured for the BOLOs in our sample was that suspects from BOLO cases were associated with significantly more crime cases recorded in ARJIS systems than suspects in comparison cases (0.9 additional crime cases, on average, when weighting by the number of suspects in each BOLO or comparison case and 0.25 when the analyzed cases were weighted equally). This is consistent with the use of BOLOs to identify crime series (described earlier). Although the analysis of this sample of cases was suggestive that BOLOs increased arrests recorded in ARJIS systems, those effects did not meet the requirements for statistical significance.

Although the controls were selected to match the highest offence, agency, and beat of the BOLO cases, there were observed differences at baseline, specifically in the number of associated crime cases prior to the focal case. We accounted for the differ-

---

[15] Parking citations were excluded from the analysis because we could not define any logical mechanism connecting them to the treatment.

Figure 3.2
Agencies Contributing Data to ARJIS Systems

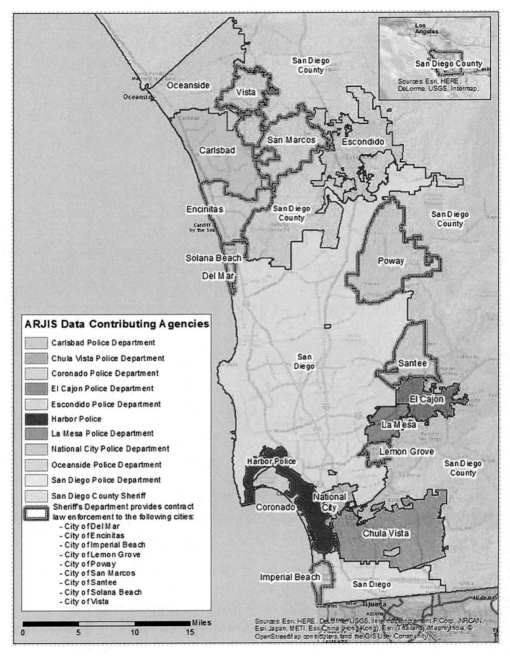

SOURCE: Provided to RAND by ARJIS.
RAND RR2099-3.2

ences at baseline via the difference-in-differences analysis, but their existence after the match may hint that other characteristics were imbalanced at baseline, too. If there are time-varying characteristics that were imbalanced between the BOLOs and matched controls, at least part of the association may be due to systematic differences between suspects in cases with BOLOs and those without. Moreover, the fact that a BOLO was issued may be an expression of greater interest in those suspects than in those who are not the subject of a BOLO, which may presage more contact with law enforcement even if the BOLO had not been issued.

Information-Sharing System Usage and Involvement in Cross-Jurisdictional Policing

In the analysis of the outcomes of ONS records as part of monitoring sex offenders, information-sharing appeared to increase the likelihood of multi-agency involvement with offenders, suggesting that sharing was achieving one of its goals to break down barriers created by jurisdictional boundaries between criminal justice agencies. Another potential outcome of improved information-sharing is addressing the fact that criminal activity crosses jurisdictional boundaries; for example, a single person or group may commit crimes in many suburbs of a metropolitan area.[16] ARJIS users employed BOLO notifications as one way to address this challenge, in an effort to identify crimes in different jurisdictions that were similar enough that they might have a common perpetrator.

The issue of "traveling criminals" or "shared offenders" has been explored in the criminological literature from a few different directions. Analyses based on criminal history data have calculated that a significant percentage of individuals who are arrested in one jurisdiction have previous arrests in other jurisdictions as well. For example, Gilmer (2010) examined arrestees in New York state and found that 16 percent of arrestees in 2008–2009 had been arrested by another agency in the state between 2004 and 2008. A similar, and much earlier, analysis in Florida examining mobility within a single year showed that more than half (53 percent) of offenders with one or more arrests in the study year (1997) had been arrested by another law enforcement agency that year, and almost a quarter (22 percent) of repeat offenders were arrested in another county that same year (Burton et al., undated, p. 6).[17] The Bureau of Justice Statistics has also examined cross-jurisdictional offending using criminal history data in a sample of states. That analysis found that, of prisoners released in 2005, 35 percent had arrests on their rap sheets from a state other than the one in which they were incarcerated (Sabol, 2012). Further work has focused on the individual level and the "journey to crime" that individuals make during their offending, in which longer

---

[16] Leipnik, Ye, and Wu (2013) provide an in-depth discussion of cross-jurisdictional issues from a historical context, including how they affect broader issues, such as the measurement of crime rates.

[17] The study also examined data for 1980, and the single-year mobility percentages were very similar (51 percent of repeat offenders had multi-agency arrests, and 22 percent had arrests in multiple counties).

distances would be more likely to cross jurisdictional boundaries (see Townsley and Sidebottom, 2010, for a review). And work in Europe has used DNA data from crime scenes to study offending patterns that are not limited to offenders who have been arrested. A study in the United Kingdom examined DNA samples submitted by individual police stations to examine crime series perpetrated by the same individuals. Half (50 percent) of the criminals in the study's data set did not travel, just more than one-third (36 percent) moved across divisional boundaries within the same police force, 7 percent offended in adjoining jurisdictions, and 7 percent offended in jurisdictions of nonadjoining police forces (Wiles and Costello, 2000, p. 26). As cited previously, similar work in the Netherlands indicated that offenders who moved across police regions had a lower probability of being caught (Lammers and Bernasco, 2013).[18]

Although multiple factors could be at play in making it difficult to apprehend traveling criminals, information-sharing might help reduce any advantage gained by offending in different geographic areas. One way to test this directly would be to measure differences in the probability of arrest, as was done in the Netherlands study, and then test whether increases in sharing made such differences smaller or disappear. Lacking the cross-cutting DNA data that provided the basis for that work, we examined this problem at the officer level, framing the question as follows: Does use of information-sharing tools increase the chance that an officer in one jurisdiction makes an arrest of someone suspected of a crime in a separate jurisdiction in the San Diego County area? The simplest case of this would be an arrest warrant issued by another jurisdiction. If an officer in one jurisdiction comes into contact with someone who has an arrest warrant issued by another jurisdiction, it would be through the search of cross-jurisdictional data sets that the officer would become aware that a warrant exists and that he or she should make the arrest. A similar dynamic could exist for cases in which investigations have not progressed to issuing warrants; for example, information in cross-jurisdictional databases about crime cases makes it possible for an investigator in one jurisdiction to contribute to clearing a case in another. Complementary to the effects detected in sex offender management, this would be a measure of the contribution of information-sharing to solving cross-jurisdictional crimes.

Because of differences in the way different jurisdictions record their data, it was not possible to definitively link crime cases in one jurisdiction to arrests in another on a large scale and in an automated way.[19] As a result, we had to build a data set that linked crime cases with identified suspects to arrests by varying criteria, which gave us a set of cases for analysis. We limited the construction of this data set to crime cases and arrests occurring in jurisdictions that contribute data to ARJIS. The strongest criterion that a case and a cross-jurisdictional arrest are related is documentation in the arrest record

---

[18] Other work by the same authors explored criminal offending across international jurisdictions in the European Union (Bernasco, Lammers, and van der Beek, 2016).

[19] This analysis is described in detail in Burgette, Stevens, and Jackson, unpublished manuscript.

submitted to ARJIS that the arrest was related to a warrant originating in another jurisdiction. If a suspect's cross-jurisdictional arrest occurring after a crime case was *not* associated with a warrant in the records submitted to ARJIS, we looked to see whether the specific highest charge (i.e., the section of the penal code related to the charge) was the same in the crime case and the arrest records. If not, we looked for a match in type and, finally, level of the charge. We always matched with the strongest of the criteria to associate a cross-jurisdictional arrest with a crime case. The data set, which covered a 64-month period, included approximately 523,000 arrests, and approximately 57,800 of those were cross-jurisdictional; thus, cross-jurisdictional arrests accounted for approximately 11 percent of all arrests during the study period.

Over the full period in which the officers covered by the analysis had recorded use of ARJIS systems in our data set,[20] we looked for a relationship between the amount of an officer's usage (e.g., did the officer do lots of ARJIS application searches or very few) and the officer's number of apparent cross-jurisdictional arrests. We captured officers' system use as completely as possible, including via desktop computers, mobile data terminals, and mobile platforms, as well as the broadest possible range of tools ARJIS provides. While not comprehensive, the tools and usage included in our measure for officer information-sharing use captured between 85 and 90 percent of ARJIS system utilization relevant to investigative activities (i.e., non–data entry or non–crime analyst usage). We used negative binomial regressions to describe count models and used logistic regression to model the probability of arrest; both models included officer-level random effects.

Because many officers did not use information-sharing tools very much, we analyzed the data on a logarithmic scale—that is, looking at the effects on cross-jurisdictional arrests from multiplicative increases in the number of instances of using different ARJIS tools (e.g., application queries, TACIDS uses). When we looked across the entire sample of potential cross-jurisdictional arrests (including warrant arrests and all matched case-arrest pairs), an increase from zero to ten queries per month in the ARJIS systems included in our analysis was associated with, on average, an estimated 0.028 more monthly cross-jurisdictional arrests per officer (from 0.164 arrests to 0.192 arrests). In other words, such increased ARJIS use increased the average estimated probability of making a cross-jurisdictional arrest in a given month from 11.7 percent to 13.1 percent (with both results highly statistically significant). With a narrower definition of a cross-jurisdictional arrest (that is, narrowing the matching criteria), the effects were in the same directions but got weaker. At the most restrictive—looking at cases that involved warrants—an increase from zero to ten queries was associated with the average number of cross-jurisdictional arrests increasing from 0.044 to 0.048,

---

[20] We analyzed each officer's use and arrest data from the first month he or she recorded use of ARJIS's systems to the last month the officer appeared in the data set, in an effort to take into account officers who started work or left their departments during the period covered by the data.

while the estimate for the probability of making a cross-jurisdictional arrest was much smaller and lost statistical significance. As with all of the analyses discussed in this report, we emphasize that the data are observational, and at least part of the observed association may reflect confounding due to unobserved factors.

Because cross-jurisdictional criminal activity represents only a portion of total criminal activity, involvement in cross-jurisdictional arrests would not be expected to necessarily be an everyday occurrence. Based on our data set built to capture cross-jurisdictional arrests, we see a positive and significant correlation between information-sharing and—admittedly small—increases in an officer's involvement in such arrests. This is consistent with the intent of sharing systems to limit the effect of jurisdictional boundaries on criminal justice outcomes. Although the effects are small, we note that they are per officer per month and therefore, in aggregate, suggest that departments with high ARJIS sharing tool utilization may be expected to have meaningfully more cross-jurisdictional policing activities. Further, in a relative sense, we believe the effects are substantial. For example, based on the full sample of arrest data, we estimate that, on average, an officer with ten queries per month would be expected to have 17 percent more cross-jurisdictional arrests per month than an officer with no utilization. Finally, because making queries requires relatively little effort, many officers average substantially more than ten queries per month. The estimated effect increases with more utilization.

Thinking About Future Systems: Designing to Capture Outcomes

As noted, to take on the evaluation challenge of measuring the effect of information-sharing on criminal justice outcomes, we used ARJIS—a regional information-sharing enterprise of multiple systems that connect many different types and sizes of criminal justice agencies across levels of government—as a real-world case study to explore different approaches and measurement strategies. Doing so produced some measures for the effect of different types of information-sharing, but the challenges encountered during the project also produced a different set of results: lessons on how systems could be designed to make this sort of effort more straightforward by building in features or addressing key problems. These lessons would make it easier to replicate and expand on the criminal justice system's ability to meet the challenge this project sought to address—linking information-sharing to justice outcomes. Yet some of the lessons could also contribute to the operational value of these systems by building in key feedback loops to improve data quality, contribute to more-useful audit and accountability information to address individual privacy and other concerns, or aid agency leadership in assessing departmental performance and making strategic decisions.

Challenges Encountered
User Roles and Their Activities

In looking at system usage across large populations of users to measure the value of the system to individual officers or analysts, one challenge we faced was the different roles, job or team structures, and variation in geographic postings that could occur. Our plans to look at the effects of information-sharing at the individual user level were complicated by the fact that some users worked as part of task forces, where someone else performed all the analytic support for the team; some worked with partners sometimes and on their own other times; and some relied on colleagues to run some searches (e.g., another officer had a mobile device and could more conveniently run a search in the field). All of these different work models created the potential for officers or analysts who were benefiting from data in ARJIS systems to do so "invisibly," from the perspective of the available analytical data sets.[21] Similar shortfalls affected our ability to explore geography-based strategies for measurement, which required data—ideally on a day-by-day basis—of where individual officers were posted so their system usage could be linked to the area of the jurisdiction where the information was being applied. In both these cases, the ability to cross-walk sharing-system use with granular data on officers' roles and postings could have helped address this issue. For some departments, such data are likely already available from other communications and personnel systems but may or may not be stored or retained in a form that is amenable to analysis.

User and System Feedback Mechanisms

One question that arose during the study was whether the data available truly documented that sharing had occurred or whether they reflected only the *possibility* of sharing; that is, were we measuring that users received information or just that it was available to them? The most straightforward example of this is our analysis of ONS records, which cause specific data about individuals, addresses, or vehicles to be more prominently displayed when a system user runs a search. Nothing in available data sets

---

[21] This issue was raised by Scott (2006, p. 130) in his examination of an information-sharing system in Florida. This effect was a major reason for one of the most significant unsuccessful measurement experiments in our study—an attempt to use the deployment of a group of new mobile devices in three departments to see how justice outcomes were affected by an increase in dosage of information-sharing capability (because the devices allowed access to ARJIS sharing applications in the field that were otherwise only available on in-car or desk computers). Allocation of the devices among officers could not be randomized, and because we could not independently control for time trends in criminal activity, simple pre-post comparison of officers' activities before and after they received a device was not meaningful. Comparison with other officers in the departments over the same period who had not received devices was a potential solution. However, beyond the lack of randomization, there was a high prevalence of officers with devices using their mobile capabilities to assist the investigative or enforcement efforts of their unequipped colleagues. Therefore, constructing a comparison group from officers who had not received the devices was impossible, because the majority of officers in the three departments received this type of second-order mobile device treatment effect to different, and unknowable, extents. As a result, while user perceptions of the new devices were positive and there were clear increases in system usage, there was no viable evaluation design to link usage to criminal justice outcomes.

could tell us whether users actually read the alerts when they were displayed. Similar questions could be asked for mechanisms like BOLO notifications. As anyone with an email inbox is well aware, some messages are opened and read immediately, some may be read some time later, and some may never be opened at all. As a result, a better assessment of the effect of that type of sharing on outcomes would be based on the number of users who actually looked at a BOLO about a case rather than the fact that an alert was sent about it.

Some of this type of data could be captured in a way that is transparent to users (e.g., like read and delivery receipts in some email systems) and therefore would not create usability burden.[22] However, other information might require changes that would affect user experience—for example, finding better ways to capture feedback *during use*. Many systems, including ARJIS's, have features that allow users to provide feedback or capture success stories. Such features have the potential to provide very useful data; for example, in Scott (2016, p. 123), this sort of success tagging was used to try to measure the "organizational distance" between the agency that was the source of data and the agency reporting a success based on its use. Similar to our effort to identify cross-jurisdictional arrests, such an organizational distance measure would be valuable for assessing how effectively a sharing system truly bridges jurisdictional boundaries. However, such success story reporting is generally done by only a minority of users, so the generalizability of the results of such an analysis is difficult to assess. Future systems could incorporate ways for users to provide feedback that are less burdensome and therefore more likely to be used. For instance, even the simple thumbs up or thumbs down that has become standard in many Internet contexts could provide a useful measure if users tagged information they viewed as particularly useful when they accessed it. Applications of such data for evaluation (e.g., whether users from one agency are frequently up-voting entries from a neighboring agency) are obvious, but they could also help provide users with feedback that could help them improve the data they entered into the information-sharing system in the course of their duties. In our interviews, some users highlighted how the detail and completeness of information that specific agencies contributed to ARJIS made that information particularly useful. If feedback systems existed that captured the fact that such information was frequently used and viewed as valuable across a region, that might create incentives to improve information quality overall.

---

[22] Straightforward ways to capture analysts' or officers' use of their own agencies' systems versus interagency information-sharing systems would also be beneficial to evaluation efforts. In our case, we were not able to gain access to participating agencies' administrative data on access to their own systems. As a result, beyond the anecdotal reports provided by the users we interviewed, we have no systematic insight into how much users' work in ARJIS systems was supplemented by searches in other systems. This issue could be addressed administratively (e.g., by maintaining such logs in a way that was readily available for analysis) but could also be addressed technologically if a common gateway existed for internal and interagency systems that could capture user choices to use one system or another. This substitution issue was also encountered by Scott (2006).

System Record and Activity Linkage

The effort to identify and measure the effects of information-sharing on criminal justice outcomes puts a premium on linking records that are related to one another—for example, the data in a field interview report that contributed to an investigation or the fact that an arrest or booking record is tied to a crime case that already existed in a local agency system. Differences in the way that agencies' individual systems are designed can significantly complicate making those links. For example, for some agencies participating in ARJIS, the record of someone's booking into jail is the "parent record" to which other data are linked, while in other agencies, the crime case is the parent record. Such differences mean that building clear links between related records is sometimes difficult. One approach to addressing this concern is to implement common data structures, standards, and interoperability initiatives to make it easier to combine data from different places, but analytic and other efforts to track links between records before data are shared could also help address the issues. Links across different components of the criminal justice system (e.g., from law enforcement to prosecutors, from the court system to corrections agencies) are also critical for assessing how sharing might affect the quality of outcomes (e.g., whether cases involving officers who use the sharing systems more have different prosecutorial, plea bargain, or court outcomes than those involving officers who use the systems less).

Another challenge in linking database use directly to outcomes at an individual level was the absence of information that cleanly linked analysts' and investigators' efforts to individual cases or justice initiatives. Some system features allow users to tag system usage to specific crime cases, although use of such features is complicated by differences in application among different agencies. The viability of such features is also challenged if making the linkage adds to user burden (e.g., a need to keep retyping crime case identifiers when logging into different systems). In seeking to build these linkages ourselves during the course of the study, we identified the limitations of the data captured by the auditing functions of some vendors' systems. For one of ARJIS's subsystems, the log files captured during searches were sufficiently cryptic that they proved impossible to use for analytical purposes—even if they met all the needs for system or database administration. Building ways for systems to help users easily make these linkages (e.g., intelligent analytical agents that make logical connections and just ask users to confirm the result) could improve auditability and accountability for use of database tools while also enabling better evaluation of their effects.

Which Administrative Data to Keep and Which to Discard

Although modern information systems capture a wide variety of administrative data, not everything can be kept. When decisionmakers consider which types of administrative data to retain, some types of information may be useful enough for evaluation to merit saving even if there is not a strong operational reason to maintain the data. In this effort, this situation arose in our attempt to measure the effects of ONASAS smart alerts sent to users by ARJIS systems. When a user cancels such an alert or it expires (because such alerts can only be placed on a record for a limited time period), the system does not maintain a log of the dates when the alert was on the record. From an operational perspective, this makes perfect sense. The alerts are intended to aid users by saving them the work of repeatedly querying the same people to see whether new information has appeared. While there are not obvious operational reasons to keep logs of when such alerts are used, the absence of such logs made it much more difficult and labor-intensive for us to attempt to measure the effects of alerts on case outcomes. We were restricted to gathering information on alerts that were in place during the study period and combining data sets from repeated sampling of active alerts to capture the dates that new alerts were placed and older ones expired. In practical terms, this restricted our sample size to the point where the attempt to evaluate that information-sharing mode was not successful.

Data Quality

While concerns about the quality of criminal justice data have been recognized for some time, our effort to use such data emphasized that improvement could not only contribute operationally but also improve the practicality and accuracy of efforts to measure those outcomes. While data hygiene issues—such as variation in names entered for suspects, incorrect dates of birth, and other identity resolution concerns—have obvious effects on investigations and other operational policing activities, they similarly affected us by making it more difficult to clearly capture the effects of sharing systems while looking at data on individual offenders' contacts with justice agencies.

Similarly, differences in how different agencies use database fields can create issues of data quality. For example, clearance of criminal cases through arrest is a measure that—though imperfect—is often prominent in assessing police department performance. Clearance rates have been part of reporting efforts, such as the Uniform Crime Reporting program, for many years. However, departments differ in how updates in case status are reflected in ARJIS systems, which is a result of variations in how and how frequently data are transmitted from agency systems to the regional sharing systems. Therefore, while we did attempt to use data on case status in ARJIS systems for analysis within the boundaries of single departments, we could not use such data in cross-agency comparisons or analyses that sought to integrate multiple agencies' data. Even differences in simpler procedures (e.g., departmental conventions for assigning case numbers and whether approaches were the same across participants in the system) could make matching cases, suspects, or arrests across different jurisdictions harder and make the results of doing so less certain.

Furthermore, database processes can lead to challenges. For example, database system changes and conversions as new technologies are implemented can create problems similar to those created by differing uses of database fields. In one of our analyses we sought to look at individuals over historical periods during which ARJIS systems had gone through significant hardware upgrades and database transition. As a result of those technology improvements, some date fields had been "lost in translation" and had to be recreated from other available data to allow the analysis to proceed.

Lessons Learned

Looking across the challenges we encountered, there are four main lessons for the design of future information-sharing systems.

First, for some of the system design issues, our results simply reemphasize the importance of initiatives that are already under way to facilitate sharing of data across agencies. For example, the Global Justice Information Sharing Initiative and the National Information Exchange Model specify data structures that, if used consistently, would address some of the issues in data quality and case-matching that we encountered. As a result, beyond the well-documented operational benefits of such standards, improving the quality and cost-effectiveness of efforts to evaluate the effects of data-sharing on criminal justice outcomes would be a nontrivial additional benefit.

Second, standardization of records across agencies, by agreeing on and adopting a unique identifier for individuals, would help address difficulties in tracking both criminal activity and actions to address that activity across jurisdictional lines. To improve the current capability to uniquely identify individuals in existing criminal justice data sets, the use of entity resolution capabilities (whether developed specifically for criminal justice or transitioned from other fields) could also improve the ability to enhance data quality and more readily link records. With increasing globalization and international human migration, the greater diversity in names, name structures (e.g., order, hyphenation), and naming conventions has increased the difficulty of identity resolution and the importance of such capabilities.

Third, where storage capabilities make it possible to do so, it would be valuable to retain more administrative data in justice information systems. Being able to link use of different system features to specific crime cases would facilitate system-level analyses like this one but would also make it possible to explore more-detailed questions. For example, measuring which types of data contribute most to solving cases could make it possible to target investments to provide the highest criminal justice value in a resource-constrained environment. Features that capture the users' roles and positions over time—from patrol officers to detectives to analysts supporting interagency task forces—not only would help in evaluation but would make it easier to craft tools to better meet users' needs. Such data would also be valuable for auditing, ensuring agency and user accountability, and helping to address concerns that government data retention and sharing raise about privacy and civil liberties.

Fourth, adding feedback mechanisms that enable linkage of specific data to outcomes could be an opportunity for systems to not just make themselves easier to assess but more useful as well. In an era when automated analytics are getting smarter and smarter, there are better ways to capture this sort of data and insight than pop-up windows that ask users to report successes or answer questions. Some features that involve users in minimally burdensome ways (e.g., thumbs up or thumbs down votes on individual data or communications) could be part of the picture, but methods that monitor usage and make connections in ways that do not burden users with more record-keeping would be better.

CHAPTER FOUR
Conclusions

Despite both widespread belief that information-sharing is important and clear logic for how such efforts could make contributions to criminal justice and homeland security success, the evaluation literature in this area is relatively limited. This effort sought to expand that body of knowledge, exploring methods to use data at a very disaggregated level—geographic areas, system users, crime cases, or individual suspects or offenders—to measure effects of information-sharing directly. Because this effort was done with a long-established cross-jurisdictional sharing system, our efforts sought to take advantage of existing variation in usage to make it possible to see how dosage of information-sharing was associated with outcomes. Readers should remain cognizant of the fundamental limitation that, despite using the strongest internal controls and comparison groups available, our results revealed associations between sharing and those outcomes rather than definitively causative effects.

The results we did obtain, despite being correlational in nature, supported the value of information-sharing in several ways. Sharing through ARJIS systems was associated with greater multi-agency involvement with specific offenders, which is consistent with the goal of sharing systems to reduce the effect of jurisdictional boundaries on agency activities and effectiveness. Data-sharing via BOLO notifications was associated with increases in the number of crime cases connected to suspects—an important outcome given the role of serial offenders in total crime burden. The dosage of use of sharing tools—measured across a large user population—was correlated with numbers and probabilities of cross-jurisdictional arrests. Although all the relationships identified were correlational because of the nature of the available evaluation designs, the results present a consistent picture of information-sharing contributing to achieving criminal justice goals.

Beyond demonstrating approaches to assess current information-sharing efforts, this effort also identified actions that could be taken going forward. Given trends toward increasing emphasis on using data to improve the effectiveness and efficiency of criminal justice agencies, our results suggest ways that new data systems could be better designed (or innovations that could be implemented in existing systems) to make the sort of analysis done here easier. In an era of tight budgets at all levels of government, making it easier and cheaper to measure information-sharing systems' contributions is likely to become more rather than less important.

Other technology trends—such as adoption of officer-worn cameras that might capture location and other data, as well as advances in analytics that may make it easier to link particular data to beneficial outcomes—have the potential to help break down some of the measurement roadblocks this analysis encountered to enable even better and more-rigorous measurement of how data help practitioners across the justice system do their jobs better. Thinking now about what data should be recorded and kept to make this sort of high-resolution analysis of the effects of criminal justice data on outcomes possible would make a down payment on a future in which justice agency leadership, analysts, and decisionmakers will know more than just that sharing data is generally valuable. They will be able to understand which data, delivered where, and delivered how contribute most to criminal justice practitioners' ability to do their jobs safely and well and to achieve the complicated set of goals that society expects them to achieve.

User Interview Questions

Our goal in interviewing users was to gather qualitative data on the use of the information-sharing tools provided by ARJIS and explore perceptions of their effects on efficiency and effectiveness. The information gathered would complement and inform the quantitative efforts to link information-sharing to criminal justice outcomes. Discussions with users also provided the opportunity to examine different work models and how they might affect evaluation design. Initial interviewees were nominated by organizations that use ARJIS systems and included individuals from different criminal justice roles. Interviewees were asked for suggestions of others whose perspectives might be good to include in the study (whether or not they were heavy users of ARJIS systems).

We completed interviews with 29 individuals whose roles varied across the criminal justice system. Of the 29, ten were analysts (seven from police departments and three from sheriff's offices), nine were detectives (all from police departments), nine were law enforcement officers (six from local police departments and three from federal agencies), and one was a probation officer. The majority (21) of the interviewees were individuals nominated by departments, and the remainder (eight) were suggested by other interviewees.

In this appendix, we reproduce the questions that we used to structure the interviews. In designing our questions, we drew on previous efforts—most notably, Zaworski's previous work on ARJIS (Zaworski, 2004, 2005), which was provided to us directly.

Structured Interview Questions

1. To start out, we would like to explore a little about how you do your work and how data or information gets brought into how you do it—not just from information systems like your agency's systems or ARJIS, but in general:
    ◦ In your job, do you mainly work alone, with a partner, or as part of a team, group, task force, or other structure?
    ◦ What are the main job tasks that you have where bringing together information to inform decisions or actions is important?
    ◦ How do you get the information or data that you need to do your job?

      [Examples, but don't prompt: querying IT systems like ARJIS or an agency [record management system (RMS)], contacting other [criminal justice] practitioners from their own agency directly (where do they get it? Accessing IT systems?), contacting practitioners from other agencies, from practitioners they work directly with (e.g., in a task force or fusion center environment), through products provided by other staff (e.g., crime analyst reports, etc.)]

    ◦ *For practitioners who don't work on their own*: Within your group/team/task force, how does information or data get brought into the group?
      i. By specific individuals who access IT systems or other sources and then distribute the information to the rest of the group [If so, why those specific people?]
      ii. By some subset of the group, but not by everyone [If so, why them?]
      iii. By everyone
    ◦ When you think about the information that you use in doing your work, what percentage of that information do you think comes from outside of your agency? Where does that information come from?

2. To get an idea of how important these systems are to what you do, we want to get an estimate of how much you use information from criminal justice IT systems (whether your agencies' or interagency information-sharing via ARJIS) in the course of doing your work.

    There are a couple different ways to think about that (we are just looking for estimates rather than exact numbers):
    ◦ What fraction of the tasks you do involve drawing data from IT systems in different ways?
    ◦ How many times in the past 5 working days did you use one of these IT systems (e.g., queried something, got an alert or BOLO from the system, etc.)?

3. Since we are looking at ARJIS as an example of a cross-jurisdiction/cross-agency information-sharing system, we want to explore your use of it versus your own agency's IT data systems (RMSs, [license plate recognition (LPR)] data systems, etc.), if applicable. Do you use ARJIS more or less than your agency's systems? What drives your decision about which system to use?

    ○ For practitioners who don't work on their own: Within your group/team/task force, who uses ARJIS?
      i.   Specific individuals [If so, why those specific people?]
      ii. By some subset of the group, but not by everyone [If so, why them?]
      iii. By everyone

    NOTE FOR INTERVIEWER: Question may not be relevant for all agencies— ARJIS is the only provider of LPR for 6 agencies and may be the RMS provider in some agencies as well.

4. If you are a regular ARJIS user, what ARJIS tools or features do you use most? If you are not a regular user, what are the barriers that keep you from using ARJIS?

    Possibilities:

    – SRFERS queries, ONS (with or without email subscriptions), advanced LPR queries, photo queries, BOLO email distribution lists, SDLaw, Global Query
    – Coplink, i2, Regional Mapping Dashboard
    – ARJIS mobile applications, TACIDS, SRFERS Mobile, CalPhoto
    – Security Center, data entry screens, eQuery/M0I11

5. How many of the last 10 [tasks—for each of the relevant tasks from lists below (e.g., for how many of the last 10 investigations, how many of the last ten citations, arrests, etc.)] you carried out did you use ARJIS?

    Possible [tasks] as relevant for the person's role:

    – Investigations
    – Citations
    – Arrests
    – Clearances
    – Identifications
    – Analyzing crime trends
    – Crime mapping or geographic crime analyses
    – Supporting individual investigations of criminal cases
    – Analysis or evaluation of policing efforts
    – Managing records

    If interviewee didn't use ARJIS for any of the last ten arrests, crime trend analyses, etc., etc., discuss why not.

6. What would you say are the "Top 3 Tasks" that you use ARJIS/interagency information-sharing for in your work?

7. Were there particular types of interagency data that were particularly important/useful for your Top 3 tasks? How was it used? Is data from ARJIS more frequently a source of new leads/information or a way to confirm information from other sources—or a mix of both?
    - Individual criminal history
    - Incident descriptive information (e.g., suspect and [modus operandi] data)
    - Open case or information on reported crimes
    - Photo data
    - Stored LPR data (whether archived or real time)
    - Real time LPR data
    - Address/location information
    - Data from outside the state/region
    - Officer notifications and alerts/wants warrants

8. Do you believe you would have been able to get these data without ARJIS? If yes, through what system/mechanism?

9. How many would have more difficult to do "as well" without the interagency data from ARJIS (e.g., linking in-custody suspects to other crimes, ability to enhance charges given individual's record?)

10. We would like to talk about whether and how you believe the access to interagency data through ARJIS affects your <u>productivity</u> as a criminal justice practitioner. We can think about this a couple of ways:
    - On an average day, does the fact that you can get access to other agencies' information through ARJIS save you time?
      - If so, how much time do you think it saves compared to other ways of doing those tasks?
    - Thinking about how productive you are now in performing the full range of tasks associated with your job, how much would that productivity go down if access to other agencies information via ARJIS wasn't available?
      - E.g., if you are able to do 10 things a day now, how many do you think you would be able to do a day without ARJIS?

11. Are there any problems or challenges that you encounter with accessing or using the data from different agencies through ARJIS?

    Areas to explore:
    - Data quality or timeliness concerns
    - Information overload/too much/duplicative information
    - Difficulties finding the information you are looking for

- System availability, ease of use or other concerns?
- Others the interviewee is aware of?

12. Finally, we would like to talk about one or more incidents/tasks/cases where interagency information from ARJIS was particularly important in getting a successful outcome or resolution—essentially a situation that could be viewed as a real success story. Are there any incidents that you were directly involved in that would be considered an ARJIS success story?

   ◦ Describe the situation for us (without any identifying information on the participants other than you, please)
   ◦ What was it about the situation that made the interagency data from ARJIS particularly important in getting to a resolution?
   ◦ What do you think would have happened if ARJIS/interagency information wasn't available? Would there have been other ways to get the interagency information if the linkage that ARJIS provides didn't exist?
   ◦ In that "world without ARJIS," how do you think the outcome of the situation would have differed?
     i. Would the chance of resolving it been different?
     ii. Would the speed of resolving it been different?

Bibliography

Agrawal, Manish, H. R. Rao, and G. L. Sanders, "Impact of Mobile Computing Terminals in Police Work," *Journal of Organizational Computing and Electronic Commerce*, Vol. 13, No. 2, 2003, pp. 73–89.

Automated Regional Justice Information System, "ARJIS TACIDS: Tactical Facial Recognition in the Field," presentation at the Law Enforcement Information Management Conference, Scottsdale, Ariz., May 22, 2013. As of May 25, 2017:
http://www.theiacp.org/Portals/0/pdfs/LEIM/2013Presentations/2013%20LEIM%20Conference%20Workshop%20-%20Technical%20Track%20-%20TACIDS.pdf

Bean, Hamilton, "Exploring the Relationship Between Homeland Security Information Sharing & Local Emergency Preparedness," *Homeland Security Affairs*, Vol. 5, No. 2, May 2009. As of August 11, 2017:
https://www.hsaj.org/articles/104

Bernasco, Wim, Marre Lammers, and Kees van der Beek, "Cross-Border Crime Patterns Unveiled by Exchange of DNA Profiles in the European Union," *Security Journal*, Vol. 29, No. 4, 2016, pp. 640–660.

Braga, Anthony A., and Desiree Dusseault, "Can Homicide Detectives Improve Homicide Clearance Rates?" *Crime & Delinquency*, e-publication, November 25, 2016.

Burgette, Lane F., Jessica Hwang, Stephanie Kovalchik, Erinn Herberman, and Brian A. Jackson, "Effects of 'Be on the Look Out' Notifications on Law Enforcement Outcomes: Evidence from San Diego County," Santa Monica, Calif.: RAND Corporation, unpublished manuscript.

Burgette, Lane F., Caroline Stevens, and Brian A. Jackson, "Associations Between Use of Information Sharing Tools and Cross-Jurisdictional Arrests in San Diego County," Santa Monica, Calif.: RAND Corporation, unpublished manuscript.

Burton, Susan E., Matthew Finn, Debra Livingston, Kathy Padgett, and Kristen Scully, *Typology of Inter-Jurisdictional Offenders in Florida*, Florida Statistical Analysis Center, undated. As of August 11, 2017:
https://www.fdle.state.fl.us/cms/FSAC/Publications-(1)/PDF/mobility_report.aspx

Casady, Tom K., Ian Cottingham, Juan Paulo Ramírez, Ashok Samal, Alan J. Tomkins, Kevin Farrell, Joseph A. Hamm, David I. Rosenbaum, and Nancy Shank, "A Randomized-Trial Evaluation of a Law Enforcement Application for Smartphones and Laptops That Uses GIS and Location-Based Services' to Pinpoint Persons-of-Interest," NCJRS 248593, January 2015.

Chen, Hsinchun, Jenny Schroeder, Roslin V. Hauck, Linda Ridgeway, Homa Atabakhsh, Harsh Gupta, Chris Boarman, Kevin Rasmussen, and Andy W. Clements, "COPLINK Connect: Information and Knowledge Management for Law Enforcement," *Decision Support Systems*, Vol. 34, 2002, pp. 271–285.

Danziger, James N., and Kenneth L. Kraemer, "Computerized Data-Based Systems and Productivity Among Professional Workers: The Case of Detectives," *Public Administration Review*, Vol. 45, No. 1, January–February 1985, pp. 196–209.

Davis, Robert C., *Selected International Best Practices in Police Performance Measurement*, Santa Monica, Calif.: RAND Corporation, TR-1153-MOI, 2012. As of April 20, 2017:
http://www.rand.org/pubs/technical_reports/TR1153.html

Devaraj, Sarv, and Rajiv Kohli, "Performance Impacts of Information Technology: Is Actual Usage the Missing Link?" *Management Science*, Vol. 49, No. 3, 2003, pp. 273–289.

Eck, John E., "Crossing the Borders of Crime: Factors Influencing the Utility and Practicality of Interjurisdictional Crime Mapping," *Overcoming the Barriers: Crime Mapping in the 21st Century*, No. 1, January 2002.

Eppler, Martin J., and Jeanne Mengis, "The Concept of Information Overload: A Review of Literature from Organization Science, Accounting, Marketing, MIS, and Related Disciplines," *Information Society*, Vol. 20, No. 5, 2004, pp. 325–344.

Federal Bureau of Investigation, *Crime in the United States, 2010*, Washington, D.C.: U.S. Department of Justice, September 2011. As of August 11, 2017:
https://ucr.fbi.gov/crime-in-the-u.s/2010/crime-in-the-u.s.-2010/clearances

Geerken, Michael, Peter Scharf, Paul Wormeli, James Sehulster, Katie Kidder Crosbie, William Stone, Heidi Unter, and Maureen Afleck, *Performance Measurement for Justice Information System Projects*, Washington, D.C.: U.S. Department of Justice, Bureau of Justice Assistance, March 2008. As of February 9, 2014:
https://www.bja.gov/publications/jis_perform_meas.pdf

Gilmer, Jim, *Shared Offenders in New York: Targeting Cross-Jurisdictional Offending Through Information Sharing*, presentation at the Justice Research Statistics Association 2010 National Conference, Portland, Me., October 28–29, 2010. As of August 11, 2017:
http://www.jrsa.org/events/conference/presentations-10/Jim_Gilmer.pdf

Harrison, Blake, *Funding Justice Information Sharing*, Washington, D.C.: National Conference of State Legislatures, 2005. As of August 11, 2017:
https://www.it.ojp.gov/documents/fundingjusticeinformationsharing.pdf

Hauck, Roslin V., *Should They Share or Not? An Investigation on the Use of Communication and Knowledge Sharing Technology in a Police Organization*, dissertation, Tucson, Ariz.: University of Arizona, 2005.

Hollywood, John S., and Zev Winkelman, *Improving Information-Sharing Across Law Enforcement: Why Can't We Know?* Santa Monica, Calif.: RAND Corporation, RR-645-NIJ, 2015. As of August 11, 2017:
https://www.rand.org/pubs/research_reports/RR645.html

Hunter, Taryn, *Overview of State Justice Information Sharing Governance Structures*, Issue Brief, Washington, D.C.: National Governor's Association, Center for Best Practices, July 2009. As of August 11, 2017:
https://www.nga.org/files/live/sites/NGA/files/pdf/0907JUSTICEINFOSHARING.PDF

Information Sharing Environment, "The Role of PM-ISE," web page, undated. As of August 11, 2017:
https://www.ise.gov/about-ise/what-ise

———, *Annual Report to the Congress: National Security Through Responsible Information Sharing*, Washington, D.C., June 30, 2012.

Inspectors General of the Intelligence Community, Department of Homeland Security, and Department of Justice, *Review of Domestic Sharing of Counterterrorism Information*, Washington, D.C., March 2017.

International Association of Chiefs of Police, "Information Sharing Initiatives," web page, undated. As of August 11, 2017:
http://www.theiacp.org/InformationSharingInitiatives

———, "IACP Issues Joint Statement with Leadership Organizations Re: Fusion Center Report," blog, October 4, 2012. As of February 7, 2014:
https://theiacpblog.org/2012/10/04/
iacp-issues-joint-statement-with-leadership-organizations-re-fusion-center-report/

Ioimo, Ralph E., and Jay E. Aronson, "The Benefits of Police Field Mobile Computing Realized by Non-Patrol Sections of a Police Department," *International Journal of Police Science and Management*, Vol. 5, No. 3, 2003, pp. 195–206.

———, "Police Field Mobile Computing: Applying the Theory of Task-Technology Fit," *Police Quarterly*, Vol. 7, No. 4, 2004, pp. 403–428.

Jackson, Brian A., *How Do We Know What Information Sharing Is Really Worth? Exploring Methodologies to Measure the Value of Information Sharing and Fusion Efforts*, Santa Monica, Calif.: RAND Corporation, RR-380-OSD, 2014. As of August 11, 2017:
https://www.rand.org/pubs/research_reports/RR380.html

Jackson, Brian A., Duren Banks, Dulani Woods, and Justin C. Dawson, *Future-Proofing Justice: Building a Research Agenda to Address the Effects of Technological Change on the Protection of Constitutional Rights*, Santa Monica, Calif.: RAND Corporation, RR-1748-NIJ, 2017. As of August 11, 2017:
https://www.rand.org/pubs/research_reports/RR1748.html

Koper, Christopher S., Cynthia Kum, James J. Willis, Daniel J. Woods, and Julie Hibdon, *Realizing the Potential of Technology in Policing: A Multisite Study of the Social, Organizational, and Behavioral Aspects of Implementing Policing Technologies*, George Mason University and Police Executive Research Forum, December 2015.

Kovalchik, Stephanie A., Erinn Herberman, Katie Mugg, and Brian A. Jackson, "Developing Outcome Measures for Criminal Justice Information Sharing: A Study of a Multi- Jurisdictional Officer Notification System for Policing Sex Offenders in Southern California," *American Journal of Criminal Justice*, Vol. 42, No. 2, 2017, pp. 275–291.

Lammers, Marre, and Wim Bernasco, "Are Mobile Offenders Less Likely to Be Caught? The Influence of the Geographical Dispersion of Serial Offenders' Crime Locations on Their Probability of Arrest," *European Journal of Criminology*, Vol. 10, No. 2, 2013, pp. 168–186.

Lammers, Marre, Wim Bernasco, and Henk Elffers, "How Long Do Offenders Escape Arrest? Using DNA Traces to Analyse When Serial Offenders Are Caught," *Journal of Investigative Psychology and Offender Profiling*, Vol. 9, No. 1, 2012, pp. 13–29.

Larence, Eileen R., *Information Sharing: Definition of the Results to Be Achieved in Terrorism-Related Information Sharing Is Needed to Guide Implementation and Assess Progress*, testimony before the Senate Committee on Homeland Security and Governmental Affairs, Washington, D.C.: U.S. Government Accountability Office, GAO-08-637T, July 2008.

———, *Information Sharing: Progress Made and Challenges Remaining in Sharing Terrorism-Related Information*, statement for the record to the Senate Committee on Homeland Security and Governmental Affairs, Washington, D.C.: U.S. Government Accountability Office, GAO-12-144T, October 2011.

Leipnik, Mark R., Xinyue Ye, and Ling Wu, "Jurisdictional Boundaries and Crime Analysis: Policy and Practice," *Regional Science Policy & Practice*, Vol. 5. No. 1, March 2013, pp. 45–65.

Lin, Chienting, Paul Jen-Hwa Hu, and Hsinchun Chen, "Technology Implementation Management in Law Enforcement: COPLINK System Usability and User Acceptance Evaluations," *Social Science Computer Review*, Vol. 22, No. 1, Spring 2004, pp. 24–36.

Linsay, Rachael, Louise Cooke, and Tom Jackson, "The Impact of Mobile Technology on a UK Police Force and Their Knowledge Sharing," *Journal of Information and Knowledge Management*, Vol. 8, No. 2, 2009, pp. 101–112.

Mitchell, Robert L., "It's Criminal: Why Data Sharing Lags Among Law Enforcement Agencies," *Computerworld*, October 24, 2013.

Moore, Mark H., and Anthony Braga, *The "Bottom Line" of Policing: What Citizens Should Value (and Measure!) in Police Performance*, Washington, D.C.: Police Executive Research Forum, 2003.

National Commission on Terrorist Attacks upon the United States, *9/11 Commission Report*, Washington, D.C.: U.S. Government Printing Office, July 22, 2004.

Noblis, Inc., *Comprehensive Regional Information Sharing Project*, Vol. 1, *Metrics for the Evaluation of Law Enforcement Information Sharing Systems*, Noblis Technical Report MTR-2006-035, Falls Church, Va., January 2007a.

———, *Comprehensive Regional Information Sharing Project*, Vol. 2, *Concept of Operations*, Noblis Technical Report MTR-2006-036, Falls Church, Va., January 2007b.

Permanent Subcommittee on Investigations, *Federal Support for and Involvement in State and Local Fusion Centers*, Washington, D.C.: U.S. Senate, Committee on Homeland Security and Governmental Affairs, October 3, 2012.

Sabol, William, *Cross-Jurisdictional Mobility in Criminal Histories*, presentation slides, U.S. Department of State, Bureau of Justice Statistics, October 30, 2012. As of August 11, 2017: http://www.crj.org/page/-/cjifiles/ICRN2_Cross-JurisdictionalMobilityinCriminalHistories.pdf

Scott, Ernest D., *Factors Influencing User-Level Success in Police Information Sharing: An Examination of Florida's FINDER System*, dissertation, Orlando, Fla.: University of Central Florida, 2006.

SEARCH, "Justice Information Sharing," web page, undated. As of August 11, 2017: http://www.search.org/get-help/training/justice-information-sharing/

Sparrow, Malcolm K., "Measuring Performance in a Modern Police Organization," *New Perspectives in Policing*, Harvard Kennedy School and the National Institute of Justice, March 2015. As of April 20, 2017: https://www.ncjrs.gov/pdffiles1/nij/248476.pdf

Straus, Susan G., Tora K. Bikson, Edward Balkovich, and John F. Pane, "Mobile Technology and Action Teams: Assessing Blackberry Use in Law Enforcement Units," *Computer Supported Cooperative Work*, Vol. 19, No. 1, 2010, pp. 45–71.

Taniguchi, Travis A., and Charlotte E. Gill, *The Mobilization of Crime Mapping and Intelligence Gathering: Evaluating Smartphone Deployment & Custom App Development in a Mid-Size Law Enforcement Agency*, Washington, D.C.: Police Foundation, 2013.

Taylor, Bruce, Bruce Kubu, Kristen Kappelman, Nathan Ballard, and Mary Martinez, *National Survey of Law Enforcement Regional Information Sharing Needs*, Washington, D.C.: Police Executive Research Forum, August 23, 2006.

Townsley, Michael, and Aiden Sidebottom, "All Offenders Are Equal, but Some Are More Equal Than Others: Variation in Journeys to Crime Between Offenders," *Criminology*, Vol. 48, No. 3, 2010, pp. 897–917.

U.S. Department of Homeland Security, *2011 National Network of Fusion Centers: Final Report*, Washington, D.C., May 2012.

U.S. Department of Justice, "Global Justice Information Sharing Initiative (Global)," web page, undated. As of August 11, 2017:
https://it.ojp.gov/global

U.S. Government Accountability Office, *Information Sharing: DHS Could Better Define How It Plans to Meet Its State and Local Mission and Improve Performance Accountability*, Washington, D.C., GAO-11-223, December 2010.

———, *Information Sharing: DHS Has Demonstrated Leadership and Progress, but Additional Actions Could Help Sustain and Strengthen Efforts*, Washington, D.C., GAO-12-809, September 2012.

———, *Information Sharing: Additional Actions Could Help Ensure That Efforts to Share Terrorism-Related Suspicious Activity Reports Are Effective*, Washington, D.C., GAO-13-233, March 2013a.

———, *Information Sharing: Agencies Could Better Coordinate to Reduce Overlap in Field-Based Activities*, Washington, D.C., GAO-13-471, April 2013b.

———, *Information Sharing: DHS Is Assessing Fusion Center Capabilities and Results, but Needs to More Accurately Account for Federal Funding Provided to Centers*, Washington, D.C., GAO-15-155, November 2014.

Wellford, Charles, and James Cronin, *An Analysis of Variables Affecting the Clearance of Homicides: A Multistate Study*, Washington, D.C.: Justice Research and Statistics Association, October 1999.

Wertheim, Kasey, "A One-Stop Shop for Crime Data: The FBI's N-DEx System, Explained," PoliceOne.com, April 1, 2016a.

———, N-DEx project manager, personal communication, October 2016b.

Wiles, Paul, and Andrew Costello, "The 'Road to Nowhere': The Evidence for Travelling Criminals," London: Home Office, Research Study 207, September 2000.

Zaworski, Martin J., "Assessing an Automated Information Sharing Technology in the Post 9-11 Era—Do Local Law Enforcement Officers Think It Meets Their Needs?" dissertation, Miami, Fla.: Florida International University, 2004.

———, "An Assessment of an Information Sharing Technology (ARJIS): Examining Its Potential Contribution to Improved Performance Through the Eyes of Street Level Officers," Washington, D.C.: National Criminal Justice Research Service, NCJRS 210487, July 2005.